The Internet of Things

Digital Media and Society Series

The Internet of Things

Mercedes Bunz and Graham Meikle

polity

First published in 2018 by Polity Press

Polity Press
65 Bridge Street
Cambridge CB2 1UR, UK

Polity Press
101 Station Landing, Suite 300,
Medford, MA 02155, USA

ISBN-13: 978-1-5095-1745-9
ISBN-13: 978-1-5095-1746-6(pb)

A catalogue record for this book is available from the British Library.

Typeset in 10.25/13 FF Scala by
Servis Filmsetting Limited, Stockport, Cheshire
Printed and bound in Great Britain by CPI Group (UK) Ltd, Croydon

For further information on Polity, visit our website:
politybooks.com

Contents

Acknowledgements

Mercedes thanks the lights for their amusing dialogues, Roomba for helping with the housework, and Toby for accepting that he has lost control of the home.

Graham thanks his connected home network – Lola, Rosie and Fin.

Introduction

What is the internet of things? The internet of things describes the many uses and processes that result from giving a *network address* to a *thing* and fitting it with *sensors*. These conjunctures of sensors, things and networks have become an increasingly important part of internet experiences. When we equip the things around us with sensors and connect them to networks, they gain new capabilities – in this book we call these *skills*. By skills, we mean a particular ability that things did not have before – such as seeing, speaking to, or tracking people. We study and evaluate these skills chapter by chapter. In particular, we explore the shifts that come with the new dimensions of communication that are enabled by the internet of things.

There's a good chance that the reader is familiar with some internet of things devices in their own daily life. Many such devices are designed for a specific use and are given a single skill – they might turn on your lights or help you count your daily steps, for instance. Others, such as the increasingly connected car, are filled with multiple sensors and network connections. And then there are the internet of things devices known as smartphones. One way of looking at smartphones is that they are general-purpose computers that can simulate many other kinds of devices – so you can use one as a piano, as a TV or as a book. To support those functions, they contain a lot of sensors. Sensors are components of a device or system that detect and communicate changes in their environment. And sensors are a crucial part of the internet of things.

But the internet of things is not just about networked sensors being fitted to things. It is also about how those things gain new skills that are expressed in new forms of communication. These new forms have been created by new interfaces, such as the *conversational technology* of a virtual assistant like Siri or Alexa. Such interfaces have become more pervasive as computing power, as cloud storage and management capacity, and as the potential to deploy algorithms in data processing, have all become both greater and cheaper. As we go through the book, we explore how both *physical* things, like smartphones, cars or human bodies, and *virtual* things, like chatbots or virtual assistants, have been incorporated into *sensing networks*.

Chapter 1, *First things*, explores *sensors* and *networks* as the two fundamental elements of the internet of things, creating a communication environment that we call sensing networks. Sensing networks of connected things are systems for *making sense* – the internet of things mediates what has not been mediated before. It is a misapprehension that the internet of things is just about connecting domestic appliances to the web. Instead of following this *Fridge Fallacy*, we show that the internet of things introduces services that disconnect the user further from a product; this fundamentally changes questions of agency. A prominent example for this is Error 53, the software bug that automatically bricked the thing genuinely precious to all of us: the smartphone. The smartphone, today used less as a phone and more as a networked computer, comes with an expanding range of sensors that have turned the device into a different kind of thing. Not just because it becomes able to sense, but also because it stays connected to the manufacturer, thereby overwriting the assumed sole ownership of the user. This chapter looks into the technical and conceptual aspects of sensors and networks as well as into the new dimensions they introduce.

Chapter 2, *Addressing things*, explores the ways in which things can be enabled to sense their locations through systems such as RFID, iBeacon or GPS. The thing that knows where it is, and where it is going, is a thing that enables new grids of surveillance and monitoring. Location can also affect how things work – a network address can make a thing function only within specific geographical borders, as in the similar way that our IP addresses today define what part of the World Wide Web we see. And if giving a network address to everything can mean that anyone can find it, this raises critical questions of security and privacy as hackers scan networks for vulnerable devices to be exploited. But the power of address can also have a utopian potential: locating and addressing a thing in space could also open up options for very different, post-capitalist models of property ownership and common use.

Chapter 3, *Speaking things*, explores the capacities of *conversational technology*. From the lukewarm jokes of Amazon's Alexa, to the nagging commands of a self-service checkout, conversations with digital technology have become normal. We talk to our phones and our phones talk back. Our cars direct us to our destinations in their out-loud voices. Conversational technology has become a daily interface for many networked things. This chapter looks at how language affects our relationships with technology, from the malfunctioning supermarket checkouts that lead people to steal, to the nomadic adventures of people who put too much trust in their car's navigation systems. It explores how some of the earliest visions of computing find contemporary expression in the networking of objects with which we can speak – such as chatbots – and how this brings with it complex combinations of agency, algorithms and anthropomorphism.

Chapter 4, *Seeing things*, explores the new capacities of connected things to see the world around them. Assisted by sensors such as lasers, radar or cameras, things have first learned to auto-focus, then to identify what is in a picture, and then to self-drive a car. Informed by the technology of neural networks, they have been equipped with the skill to interpret information, thereby giving it meaning, although not always the correct one – they may mistake a baby playing with a toothbrush for a young boy holding a baseball bat, or fail to recognize a black person in an image. This chapter explores how sight imbues connected things with a new agency, for which programming must be held accountable in the future.

Chapter 5, *Tracking things*, explores the use of connected sensors to monitor, measure and quantify the individual's health. Health-tracking devices such as the Fitbit, health-monitoring apps designed to work with major platforms such as Android, and the increasing integration of health technologies and tracking sensors into smartphones are driving changes in the ways that many people look after themselves. The personal, the intimate and the pathological are now all mediated with others. One's daily activities and routines, diet and exercise habits, locations and movements, sleeping patterns and sexual activity, intake of caffeine or sugar, of alcohol or nicotine, of proscribed substances or prescribed medication – these all become knowable information to audiences that may not always be recognized or expected. Such detailed information has not been mediated until now. As the biological and the technological converge in those new networked systems, they redraw distinctions between public and private information, bringing new kinds of concerns about surveillance and security.

Addressing, speaking, seeing, tracking – these capabilities built into networked objects show that the internet of things has already become much more than just a simple internet-connected device. Instead, new and different uses of networked digital media, and new and different experiences, have been introduced for both public and personal communication. To examine those aspects, we draw upon a range of theoretical and philosophical perspectives on technology and communication. We use the methods of historical analysis, to study how change occurs in society, combined with Critical Discourse Analysis (Fairclough 2003, Machin & Mayr 2012, Hansen & Machin 2013, Wodak 2013) – the latter most explicitly in chapter 4 and chapter 5. By examining word choices and patterns, organization and assumptions, as well as the use of image and design, we look at what contributes to the meanings of texts about the internet of things that have been written by companies at its heart. Viewing language as a form of social practice, we look at texts produced by firms involved in the internet of things such as Fitbit, Tesla or Google, and study how they suggest meanings for their new inventions, and how they introduce certain ideas of agency and power into our discourse.

In using both methods, we aim to explore the specific social and political qualities of the internet of things, and to get a deeper understanding of the newly acquired skills of things from the perspective of communication. We focus on the corporate applications of these skills, and with them the new roles that users have been given. And we aim to show that this is a topic that media and communication scholars need to take seriously. Other work that addresses the internet of things is often business-focused (such as Greengard 2015) or uncritically enthusiastic about the economic possibilities of sensing networks. Further contributions come from very different fields, addressing technical security (Dhanjani 2015), politics (Howard 2015) or design aspects (Sterling 2005, Rose 2014). This book, in comparison, emphasizes communication. We explore the specifics of sensing networks and their communicative capacities, in order to better understand the social dimensions of the internet of things.

The book emphasizes throughout that the internet of things is built on already familiar technologies, which have been developed further. To describe its development, we often use examples that have attracted some media attention and that readers may recognize. In a disruptive environment such as digital technology, it is only natural that some of those examples will soon be out of date. But those examples should be distinguished from the *concepts* that they illustrate. Those concepts describe more fundamental shifts within the field of communication, such as those caused by recording devices and sensing networks, by conversational technology or algorithmic sight.

Of course, the internet of things is an industrial formation, and is bound up in part with questions of automation, manufacturing, agriculture, retail and transportation (Government Office for Science [UK] 2014). It also extends well into economic sectors once considered *knowledge* or *creative* industries. In their book about the future of work, Robert McChesney and John Nichols survey the internet of things and the claims for its economic potential. They adduce claims such as that of Cisco Systems that the internet of things will generate savings and revenues of $14 trillion by the year 2022, and conclude by warning: 'A large share of these savings will come by eliminating jobs' (2016: 94). Others, like Nick Srnicek and Alex Williams (2015), demand to read the same recent high-tech developments as a step towards a post-capitalist economy capable of achieving a utopian world without work, for which we should get organized. To those authors, the rapid automation of logistics such as the internet of things turns into the possibility of a globally interconnected system that could be used as a post-work platform (2015: 178).

Our aim with this book, however, is to develop an account of the internet of things from a different perspective – the perspective of communication and media. So this book, above all, approaches the internet of things as *a matter of communication and meanings*. Technological systems embody ideas about the ways in which we organize ourselves and each other, and they also provide the means for us to make meanings about that social organization. Understood in this way, a book about the internet of things is also a book about its human usage. Through looking at the capabilities of sensing networks, this is a book about the human dimensions of technology and about the technological dimensions of the human.

1

First things

The phones had been working fine. But then came the update. And with the update came a new error message – Error 53. This message indicated that the Apple iPhone 6 would no longer work and could not be fixed. Thousands of smartphone owners were confronted with this message telling them that their phones could not be restored. Error 53 had been triggered by a software update, which could sense if a user had turned to a non-Apple employee to repair the phone's touch-sensor home button. For whatever reason – urgency, availability, travel abroad, simple preference – the phone had not been taken to the Genius Bar of one of the company's Apple Stores, but to some other shop to be repaired. When the phone's new internal security check detected unfamiliar parts used in its repair, it automatically bricked the phone in a way that rendered it irretrievable.

Apple described this in an announcement (2016a) as a security feature, designed to make phone theft more difficult. The bricking of thousands of iPhones may have been an unintended consequence of the software feature. But it also kept the users dependent on the manufacturer. Although the company moved quickly to update their iOS software, the incident revealed that the users did not, as they had imagined, own the expensive phone in their hands, however intimate a relationship they had developed with their devices. Instead, the episode revealed that, in practical terms, the phones were very much under the control of Apple. Error 53 also revealed the extent to which daily media use now involves complex relationships between networked objects, fitted with sensors that detect and communicate change in their environment.

Error 53 is an example of the internet of things. Some readers may be surprised that a book about the internet of things should open its first chapter with a story about a smartphone. They may imagine instead that the internet of things is about fridges or factories or retail supply chains. But we want those readers to consider the smartphone as a different kind of thing – not just as a phone, but as a networked object fitted with many sensors. Other readers may expect to read that the internet of things is a future phenomenon that has not yet arrived – and may never do – rather than the smartphones that have been in their pockets for a decade or more. Like all technological formations, the internet of things manifests complex patterns of both adoption and adaptation. And the object whose adoptions and adaptations most clearly illustrate the transformations that happen when our things become networked and learn to sense the world around them is the smartphone.

To think of the smartphone as primarily a *phone* recalls McLuhan's observation that we tend to explain new phenomena by reaching for a comparison with the past. 'We look at the present through a rear-view mirror' (McLuhan & Fiore 1967: 74–5). Instead, consider the smartphone as a networked computer that has an expanding range of sensors built into it. Sensors are components that allow the device to detect changes in its environment or to respond to stimuli (Kalantar-zadeh 2013, Gabrys 2016). And because your device is networked and identifiable, so are you. Your smartphone locates where you are, detects which direction you are heading, and records how fast you are moving to get there. Its touch-screen uses capacitive sensors that detect the user's fingertip gestures. It continually listens to its ambient environment, so that when you speak to its digital assistant – for example by saying *OK Google* or *Hey Siri* – it is ready to respond. What we call the phone's cameras are digital image sensors that detect and interpret light. Depending on the model, your phone might contain a fingerprint or a retina sensor, used to unlock the device and responsive only to the unique physical characteristics of the individual user. There may be a proximity sensor that shuts off the app screen when you're holding the phone close enough to your face to make a call. There may be a barometer that can sense air pressure and elevation. There may be a moisture indicator that detects when the device has been submerged in water. There may be an ambient light sensor that adjusts the brightness of the screen. There may be a magnetic field sensor to operate the inbuilt compass app and the device's location services used to define your precise physical position – these find uses in art museum walkthrough tours that detect which painting the user is looking at, as well as for hook-up apps that help the user find where that specific person is in that busy nightclub. There may be an accelerometer that adjusts the orientation of the screen from portrait to landscape as the device is tilted. Or there may be a more complex 'three-axis gyro' sensor that detects rotation around any axis, enabling precise location uses or sophisticated gaming or augmented reality effects through which objects on screen can rotate as the device itself rotates. Your smartphone also connects you to countless other networked things, and your phone can detect and respond to these – it reacts to real-time traffic updates and informs you about breaking news. To see the smartphone as just a kind of *phone* is to look at it in the rear-view mirror. Its many sensors, its internet connectivity and its access to data have turned it into a new kind of thing.

This is a book about why and how this environment of connected things and sensors matters. Any object or device can now be linked to digital communication networks – your phone, your watch, your car, yes, but also beehives and basketballs, razors and rocks, stoves and sex toys. Things have become media, able to both generate and communicate information. Since 2008, internet-connected *things* have outnumbered the world's human population (Pew Research Center 2014: 2). According to tech consultancy firm Gartner (2017), 8.4 billion networked things were in use by 2017, an increase of 31 per cent on the year before. The European Commission (2016: 2) estimates that more than 26 billion things will be connected by 2020. A widely cited report by Cisco goes further and claims that 50 billion devices will be connected to the internet by 2020 (Evans 2011: 3; see also Pew Research Centre 2017: 41). And once connected, any thing can become a part of further networks and be used to circulate information. More than this, a connected thing can be designed to sense its environment and create information about what is happening there.

Your fitness wristband records details of your heart rate, your daily movements and your sleeping habits, circulating these and many other intimate insights between devices and servers. Your phone's location services power apps such as Citymapper that allow your partner to check where you are while crossing the city to meet you. While you are at work, your vacuum cleaner moves through your kitchen, pausing to rotate in a circle for extra effect when it senses dirt. Your car warns you that there's bad traffic a few miles ahead and self-drives itself on an alternative route home, thanks to street lamps equipped with sensors that infer traffic patterns from air pollution. The internet is no longer just about connecting computers – now, equipped with sensors and connectivity, every single thing can be connected. Once networked, things have become able to record and process, to store and circulate information. From cars to vacuum cleaners, things can now see where they are going, what is in their way, and what they can do about that. Household objects are now able to listen to what you say, interpret your natural speaking voice when you ask them to switch the light on, or respond to your comments with a joke. Things have started to communicate and to sense the world around them.

Sensing networks

The developments we address are not just about *things in general*, about adding inert objects such as kettles or umbrellas to the World Wide Web; they are also about networking many different kinds of sensors that can detect and communicate change in their environments. So as well as the term *internet of things*, we also use the term *sensing networks* to describe those phenomena. Sensors generate and circulate information in ways that turn them into actors in networks of communication. Networked sensors mean that the sensed information can be compared with other data to calculate a response. Networked sensors are being used to construct an environment in which the sensing and locating, the measuring and responding, the communication capacities of a convergent device like the smartphone, are dispersed and embedded across the entire environment around us.

Sensors are common in daily life, from smoke detectors to pregnancy tests, from shop doors that open automatically to lights that switch on when we enter the room (Kalantar-zadeh 2013, Andrejevic & Burdon 2015, Gabrys 2016). There are lots of different kinds of sensors in the internet of things. What they all have in common, despite their differences, is that they are components of a device or a system that detect and communicate their environment. Sensors may measure or respond to physical stimuli, such as the fingerprints, retina structure or voice patterns of a specific individual – your own phone may use these kinds of sensor to let you unlock it. Sensors may detect changes in their location, position, orientation, elevation, or speed or distance of movement. They may detect changes in moisture levels or atmospheric pressure, react to the presence of liquid or gas, record changes in the chemical composition of an entity, or respond to altered levels of heat or light or sound. What all of those sensors do is detect and record change, and circulate information and messages. They create and communicate data about the world and those in it. *Sensors are media of communication.*

So sensors are one fundamental element of the internet of things. Another is that those sensors are connected to *networks*. In this context, the term *network* does not only mean that things are connected, thereby becoming 'smart'. The word *network* also invokes a number of different conceptual aspects that we draw upon in this book. As Bruno Latour has argued (2005: 129), there are three very different aspects that need to be considered when it comes to networks. There is the *infrastructural* sense, as in train or electricity networks. There is the *organizational* sense, in which markets, firms and states relate to each other. And there is also the *conceptual* sense, in which tracing and inferring networks is a method of analysis. In Latour's own words: 'Network is a concept, not a thing out there. It is a tool to help describe something, not what is being described' (2005: 131). In this book, we draw upon all three of these dimensions of *network* – to describe infrastructure, to describe organizations, and also to make connections between different kinds of actors and groups that come together to create or use technologies for communication. Towards the end of this chapter we return to the Error 53 example and examine it as a network of relationships between human and technological actors.

Besides Latour, the work of Manuel Castells has also been pivotal in bringing the word *network* to the centre of contemporary analysis of media and communication, particularly through his *Information*

Age trilogy of the late 1990s and his later book *Communication Power* (2009). So central is the term to his analysis that, as academic Mark Graham once pointed out on Twitter (2014), *Communication Power* has one short sentence that manages to include the word *network* seven times (you can find it on p. 426). In Castells' analysis, networks are structures for the processing of flows of information. The globalization of finance and industries, the rapid development of digital communications systems and the pervasive use of information technologies have allowed for the creation of the infrastructure for a *network society* (Castells 2000, 2009). In this analysis, network structures increasingly predominate over hierarchical ones, because networks can be easily reconfigured, can be expanded or contracted to respond to changing circumstances, and can survive damage or alterations to individual parts of a network (2009: 23). Castells describes how resources of political, financial and social power are increasingly exercised through network structures of organization – as is resistance to these forms of power by contemporary social movements that draw both on identity politics and on opposition to neoliberalism (Castells 2004, 2012). With this Castells brings together the different aspects of *network* discussed above – the infrastructural, the organizational and the conceptual senses of networks. He describes networks that have specific forms of organization as a result of particular technological developments. In this as well as in the next chapters of this book, we extend this approach further onto the internet of things. We examine newly developed infrastructural and organizational networks that equip things with new skills, in order to see how those skills allow for new forms of organization and power. And we consider how networked things also provide a resource for political alternatives – for example, by allowing new ways of communal usage of technological resources.

Such shifts follow from things being linked to networks. The technical development crucial for the internet of things is that it has become possible to link *anything* to networks. Networked things rely on many different communication protocols, such as Bluetooth, ZigBee, Near-Field Communication (NFC), Wi-Fi, Z-Wave, LoRa, Sigfox and others, as well as mobile telecommunication networks, including the impending rollout of 5G. A further crucial development is the introduction of internet protocol version 6 (IPv6). IPv6 became necessary when the internet began to fill up in the first decade of the twenty-first century. Back in the 1970s, the computer scientists developing the internet had assumed the need for no more than a few billion network points (on the early development of the net and the key choices that informed how it developed, see Abbate 2000, Leiner et al. 2000, Castells 2000, 2001). But by 2011, the final available blocks of IPv4 addresses were allocated to domain name registry agencies. So its successor IPv6 was designed to take a while to fill up. IPv6 allows for 3.4×10^38 addresses. That's 340 trillion trillion trillion internet addresses, or 340 followed by 36 zeros, which should keep us going for a while (Bratton 2015).

The availability of protocols such as Bluetooth or ZigBee, and the dramatically increased capacity of IPv6, enable the potential networking of essentially anything at all. This may sound like a very different internet from that of cat videos on YouTube and holiday photos on Facebook. But, in fact, it can be seen as an extension of that internet across our entire environment. Like those cat videos and holiday photos, the sensing networks of the internet of things are a matter of communication and mediation. They concern the creation and distribution of information, and they concern the interpretations of that information that we call *meanings*. So the internet of things should not only be seen as a rarefied domain of engineers, industrial designers and urban planners. It is also the domain of those of us whose concern is the uses of networked digital media for both public and personal communication, and those of us who study the many ways in which media are used for purposes of control or communion, of entertainment or information. The internet of things should be seen as a major development for the field of media and communication studies. It is an internet that offers a rich area of study to humanities and social science scholars of communication.

Communication is the making of meanings. Research in communication and media tends to focus on human communication, where meanings are produced by the circulation of messages between people. Messages may be exchanged one-to-one (as in an exchange of letters between lovers), or few-to-many (as in a TV news broadcast), or many-to-many (as in the fervour of a trending Twitter hashtag). In each of these cases, the focus is generally on the human beings who are producing, circulating and interpreting the message. But now that things can be networked and equipped with sensors that allow them to detect and record information about their environment, they too can create data about the world and those in it, and they too can circulate it. Communication now *originates* from networked things. Having been taught to sense the world around them and programmed to talk to people directly, things have been put in the roles of senders and receivers of information. The human-to-human communication of those love letters, TV broadcasts and tweets is now complemented by human-to-machine, machine-to-human and machine-to-machine communication.

Networked things do not simply respond to a stimulus or command – they produce information that can be distributed through digital networks for analysis and interpretation. They *communicate*. With this, the internet of things becomes not just a means of collecting or recording data, but enables systems of interpretation and judgement through programmed algorithms that interpret data. *Is the air quality OK? Are you overweight? Is that large object through the windscreen a reversing truck?* Sensing networks of connected things are systems for *making sense*. They are used not just to record data, but to make meanings as well, and for this reason this book sees internet of things technologies as systems of mediated communication. Sensing networks are media.

The Fridge Fallacy

For many people, the term *internet of things* is perhaps mainly associated with novelty kitchen gadgets such as the internet fridge. This misapprehension that the internet of things is just about connecting domestic appliances to the web is what we call the *Fridge Fallacy*. In this, the internet fridge is usually described as one that will alert its owner when they are running out of milk – perhaps by texting a selfie of its contents as a prompt for further shopping, perhaps by going ahead and ordering the milk itself. The internet fridge has been launched and re-launched so many times that it is now at once both futuristic and retro. Actually available since the turn of the century but without ever finding a popular market, internet fridges still feel like vapourware – a running joke for tech journalists, like jetpacks or flying cars.

But while they are the paradigm case of the novelty networked appliance, the Fridge Fallacy is not just about fridges. For every domestic utensil or appliance, there is now a connected version on the market. There are coffee-makers and kettles, networked wirelessly and controlled by smartphone apps. There is a smart iron, a $700 networked juicer, a wine bottle with wireless connectivity, and an internet-enabled kitchen pedal bin. There is a smart frying pan that uses heat sensors and sends notifications to a smartphone app to tell you when your pancake needs to be flipped. There is a Bluetooth-enabled umbrella. There are clothes pegs packed with sensors and linked to your phone, and you can use them to hang out your networked vibrating jeans. There is a candle whose flame is ignited or extinguished through a phone app. There is an 'intelligent cup', called the Pryme Vessyl, that 'automatically tracks and displays your personal hydration needs'. There is a sofa with an app. There is a smart mattress fitted with impact sensors that is marketed as a device to detect infidelity, and will notify the user that it senses someone is impacting their mattress at an unexpected time of day. There are *power sockets* controlled by phone apps. (Many of these examples are archived on the Tumblr blog *Fuck Yeah Internet Fridge* and the Twitter feed @internetofshit – swearing and the internet of things seem to pair more naturally than many Bluetooth devices.)

As Andrew Ross (1994) has pointed out, we are increasingly surrounded by inanimate objects which promise to outsmart us – smartphones, smart homes, smart cards, smart bombs. Yet as our things become smarter, it doesn't necessarily follow that we do too. The paradox of the smart device is that its user doesn't need to understand it. We invent and design it in that way, as Gilbert Simondon (2017: 16) remarked:

> . . . the machine is the stranger; it is the stranger inside which something human is locked up, misunderstood, materialized, enslaved, and yet which nevertheless remains human all the same . . .

Digital things often deny their technical complexity in order to meet the acceptance of the user. The more user-friendly something is, the less the user has to understand anything about how it works (Bunz 2015). Instead, we point and click, drag and drop, pinch and swipe. A push-button answer to a given problem can be a wonderful thing, but there is also a sense in which it deliberately de-skills and disempowers the user. It is technology that addresses the user not as an adult but as a child – a problem that seems to prevail.

Think of the gulf between the expectations placed on the user by the Raspberry Pi and by the Apple iPad – the former, a printed circuit board with a processor that is intended for learning to create and program for oneself; the latter, a closed proprietary system that is intended to allow the simple usage of other people's computing applications. The Raspberry Pi is a challenging environment that the user learns to understand and use by developing it for themselves. Using a Raspberry Pi makes the user smarter. In contrast, the Apple iPad's user-friendly touch-screen point-and-click entertainment platform, on which the user downloads and interacts with apps approved for sale and consumption by Apple, saves its user the trouble of learning or understanding anything about how it works. As computer user interfaces (CUI) from iPad to Siri learn to function more seamlessly and understand their users better the more they are used, we become less and less aware of their rules of functioning. This does not necessarily need to be the case. So rightly Benjamin Bratton asks: 'What if there were a new version of Siri in which the more it was used, the more its user understood about how the whole CUI stack works, not less?' (Bratton 2016: 316).

Not understanding how a device works brings problems. This is dramatized in one episode of the TV series *Mr Robot*, in which a character enters her expensive smart home to find that all of its networked appliances are out of control. The burglar alarm won't turn off, the home cinema system turns on by itself, the lights in her indoor pool fail, the music streaming system cuts in and out at deafening volume, the shower thermostat resets and scalds her, the heating system refuses to respond to her commands. '*What am I supposed to do? Nothing is working*', she yells at a support helpline on the phone. '*Unplug what? Everything is inside the walls. That's how it was installed when I bought the smart house package.*' In this dystopian vision of the internet of things, daily domestic life depends on proprietary systems that are beyond the reach of their users – user-friendly environments become user-hostile. The fictional *Mr Robot* scenario finds real-life expression in numerous videos on YouTube, in which exasperated people are unable to switch off their smart smoke detectors. As veteran internet commentator Howard Rheingold observed in a survey of expert opinion on the internet of things: 'We will live in a world where many things won't work, and nobody will know how to fix them' (Pew Research Center 2014: 12).

Uncooperative devices and things are certainly a part of the internet of things. But we should not assume that the internet of things is just a means to sell novelty appliances – that assumption is part of the Fridge Fallacy. Connected household appliances are always more than just *products*. Once networked, things gain another really important aspect – *data*. It is the access to data that provides the internet of things with specific skills, one of them being to evaluate and measure its own users. Here we should recall the Web 2.0 business model, whose characteristics were first articulated by Tim O'Reilly (2005). In the wake of the first dot.com crash, he noted some of the features common to internet companies that were still doing well in the early twenty-first century. One of these was their use of what he called an 'architecture of participation'. This means that what users do with a software service goes on to become part of that service for others. Actual use of the service contributes new data to the database that powers the service; this increases the value of that service both for its users and for the company behind it. So, for example, as users upload ever more videos to YouTube, the platform becomes an ever more attractive destination for others because it has ever more content; or as users search on Google, their search histories and choices inform the algorithms that will be used to further refine future search results for other people. In both these examples, what the user is contributing through this 'architecture of participation' is data. This can take the form of content (uploading a new video), behaviour (which choice is made from clickable options) or metadata (where the user is, what kind of device they are using, the associated traces in their developing digital history). The more that users contribute to the platform, the bigger its database becomes, and the greater commercial value the firm can derive from advertisers and marketers who want to use those data.

For the western world, this has led to an oligopoly of just a handful of firms, as those with the biggest databases become hard for others to catch. In the second decade of the twenty-first century, the internet in the west is largely dominated by an oligopoly of the big five: Amazon, Apple, Facebook, Google and Microsoft. It is true that firms come and go within such hierarchies – Yahoo remained a big player for many years beyond its heyday in the 1990s, followed by a long decline; Twitter is perpetually described by analysts as in a state of crisis, despite its hundreds of millions of dedicated users; and so on and on. It is also true that these western corporations do not have the whole global internet to themselves – China, notably, has its own dominant ecosystem of tech firms, with Tencent and Alibaba pre-eminent. And beyond the big five, there is also a separate hierarchy of telecommunication and broadband providers, and several tiers of big players in hardware, software and communications products and services. The internet of things has already generated a great many diverse start-up firms. But the key point is that the database business model leads to a small handful of very big winners. And as these firms extend their presence into the internet of things, data strengthen their position further.

The social media activities of the biggest internet firms have brought with them new cultural practices that have become central to the daily lives of hundreds of millions of people – friending and following, commenting and tagging, liking and sharing. Each of these practices is also a revenue stream for the major firms. These firms turned the address books and photo albums, the likes and dislikes, the opinions and emotions of their users into data to be used in the advertising business. The internet of things takes this further. Now firms reach past address books and photo albums, and into their users' shopping lists, domestic appliances, cars, beds and bodies. The internet of things mediates what has not been mediated before – what you eat, what you drink; how fast you walk, how fast you drive; where you go, and how you get there; who you meet, and what you do together; your heart rate, your hormone cycle, your blood alcohol level; what time you turn the washing machine on, how long you spend in the shower, how often you vacuum your bedroom, whether you leave the lights on when you're out, what direction you like to face when you sit down on the train. Each of these new intrusions into daily life represents a new source of data for such firms. All of this is information that has not been mediated before – and this is exactly why firms invest in the internet of things. They reach out into the fabric of daily digital life, through fitness trackers and smart TVs, in order to gain access to new streams of data. Daily life becomes reimagined as a loyalty card scheme. Should all of this powerful information be left to private companies alone?

Some agency, no intention

Earlier in this chapter, we identified some of the skills and capabilities that things have been equipped with through being connected to digital networks. Here, we want to focus on the fact that with those skills, things also acquire new and different capacities to act (Bunz 2016). Through being networked, they have gained *agency*. That things can have agency, of course, is nothing new. The agency of things has been discussed in the academic discourse for quite a while. It has not only been linked to Heidegger's (2001) early philosophical approach towards things, but also discussed in sociology and anthropology (for example Gell 1998, Latour 2005). Latour (2005) introduces an agency of things in his early work on actor-network theory, discussing the active social role of things. By the beginning of the twenty-first century, the agency of things had finally attracted attention far beyond sociology and Latour. In the US, Bill Brown launched the research field of 'thing theory' with several studies and books (2001, 2004, 2015) often exploring the agency of things in artistic work or of artistic work. Recently, further publications of other authors have followed. In *Entangled*, Ian Hodder (2012) explores things as an active entity focusing on the effect the materiality of things has on our relationship to them. In *The Universe of Things*, Stephen Shaviro (2014) aims to introduce a new rise of material thought by exploring things and objects as their own entities. And before those books, Daston (2007), Ingold (2010) and Miller (2010) had already made it obvious that our time was theoretically concerned with the agency of things.

Discussing the agency of things, however, gets more complicated, when it comes to the internet of things. In philosophical discussions, a 'thing' has a long tradition of being defined as independent. A thing, as Heidegger famously put it, 'stands on its own' and is considered to be 'self-supporting' (2001: 165). Things are artefacts, made or used by human beings, but they show 'the self-supporting independence of something independent' (p. 164). This independence is breached when things get networked, a development about which Heidegger would surely have been aghast. Because by being networked, your watch, your car, your vacuum cleaner have become products that are never finished – they are now constantly updated and constantly process data. Connected things, as Simondon foresaw, become a new category. When they enter a 'network reality' (Simondon 2012: 11), the agency of the internet of things becomes twofold. It does not only lie in their materiality. Other than in thing theory, we need to look *beyond* this material agency to their technicality: by being wired, things are gaining new skills. They are now tracking, speaking, seeing and addressing. For this, they are constantly processing information, and this new technical regime brings its own discourse. Regarding the agency of things, one aspect of that discourse in particular needs further attention – that of technological determinism.

The term 'technological determinism' is generally used for a position that assumes it is technology alone that drives social develop-ment, thereby defining the structures of a society as well as its cultural values. It reads technology as an external force that acts upon society, rather than as an expression of economic or political interests. Ever since Raymond Williams (1974) highlighted this in his critique of Marshall McLuhan (1964), to accuse another of technological deter-minism has been something of a winning move in any argument about the role of technology in media, communication and cultural studies. In these fields, a determinist position on technology is still most often associated with McLuhan, and his provocation that 'the medium is the message' (1964: 7).

There may be no position in the field of communication that draws more consistent objections than technological determinism – objec-tions that are endlessly restated as each new position on technology has to define itself in relation to this determinist paradigm. Thinkers as diverse as Ellul (1964) and Kittler (1999) are found to fall within the determinist ambit. It can also be found as a common position in many writings about digital technology, notably the 1990s *Wired* magazine discourse, which became known as 'the Californian Ideology' (Barbrook & Cameron 2015). It persists in the writing of some of the key figures of that period, as in the title of former *Wired* editor Kevin Kelly's book, *What Technology Wants* (2011). And, in a more nuanced way, it is still drawn upon in research about today's digital technology: for example in Benjamin Bratton's recent comprehensive study, which writes about 'a technological totality as the armature of the social itself' (2015: xviii), while at the same time insisting that this totality should not be understood as a completely closed system. Not very surprisingly, entire fields of social enquiry have developed to position themselves in opposition to this determinist paradigm, such as the Social Construction of Technology approach (MacKenzie & Wajcman 1999).

For our part, when discussing the agency of technology, we often refer to things in an active way. So we can anticipate some readers charging us with technological determinism. At various points in this book, we write for example that *things have started to communicate and sense the world around them.* We claim that *the things around us have started to speak.* And we suggest that *connected things have learned to see with their own eyes.* This is because things have functions. As Latour points out, it is uncontroversial to use language such as *kettles boil water* or *knives cut meat* (Latour 2005: 71). The kettles and knives are doing things, they have an active role, they have agency – what they do *not* have is *intention*. This distinction between *agency* and *intention* is important in assessing the role of technology within networks of social relations. The distinction can be described as follows: technology has an effect, but no intention. It has an agency, but does not follow an interest of its own. It can be extended and completed in very different ways, but the question of which of those ways is made real is a political decision.

To us, a technological development is therefore always a contest between contending forces, interests and possibilities. The technical possibilities of a technology as much as the aspirations of design, the constraints of regulation, the imperatives of the marketplace and the responses of users, are all factors in the contested developments of technologies (Meikle & Young 2012: 20–34, Bunz 2014: 54). This book is as much concerned with the social, economic and political interests that try to shape the internet of things as it is with understanding and studying the potentials of such new technologies. For it is often social, economic and political interests that select, research, invest in and promote certain technical possibilities over others to decide which of the many possible internets of things will become realized. And this is exactly why we think that the technological agency with which the internet of things confronts us needs attention. So in this book we try to find ways of discussing questions of technology and agency while not taking a determinist stance.

Commercial potential is often a significant driver of what turns out to be a dominant technology, even where this has other disadvantages against its alternatives. There are examples of this from deep in the history of today's internet fridge. For example, in a classic piece of technology criticism, Ruth Schwartz Cowan (1985) explained why the fridge hums in the middle of the night. That hum is a consequence of the refrigerator's electric motor. But until 1925, in the US, where the technology was mainly developed, the gas fridge was actually more widespread. The gas-powered fridge was almost silent – it didn't hum. It was easy to maintain and relatively cheap. None of those points is true of the electric fridge. But the electric fridge prevailed, and the gas fridge is today a rare technology. Cowan's argument is that key corporations that invested in the electric fridge – General Electric, Westinghouse, General Motors – were able to implement their own priorities to a degree that the gas fridge start-ups couldn't match. Those big corporations were involved across the entire electricity industry, and it was very much in their interests to see that fridges developed in that direction too. They had the resources to develop and market their preferred technology more aggressively and successfully than did the less-established companies making the gas fridge. So the domestic ubiquity of the electric fridge was not determined technologically, but through economic relations.

Technical possibilities taken up by companies also often lead to technical realities, for which the internet of things itself is an excellent example. In its early years, the technical extension of the internet across our physical environment was discussed as a fascinating phenomenon soon to come. But the actual applications that were offered for that physical environment were rarely convincing. This led to the Fridge Fallacy. And no wonder. An expensive fridge that reminds you to buy milk is not the killer app that everyone feels they have to get. Today, there are modestly more useful connected things such as lights that are remote-controlled by a voice-activated digital assistant or a smartphone app, but these too are hardly a must-have. It was the possibility of accessing and exploiting more of consumers' personal data, together with the new technical feasibility that lured one company after the other into developing internet of things applications. 'Technical reality lends itself remarkably well to being continued, completed, perfected, extended', notes Gilbert Simondon (2012: 13). If technology lends itself to being continued, it is therefore important to understand what aspects are being further developed and which ones are passed by, in order to evaluate them critically. This is why we study the technical reality of the internet of things as much as the political or economic interests that traverse it.

To clarify our position on agency and technology further, let's return to the Error 53 case, with which we began this chapter. It was a very internet of things event – one that revolved around remotely controlled sensors and identifiable, networked objects. Those touch ID sensors detected the user's fingerprint, and matched it with a deposited one that had been stored and encrypted directly on the phone by a security processor called *Secure Enclave*. To be secure, they were paired directly with each phone. When Apple added a new feature to the iOS software, the pairing of the sensor with the phone meant that the new code would then revalidate itself with Apple, thereby checking if someone had tampered with the sensor (while breaking into the phone, for example). A failed revalidation would cause the security processor to shut the phone down – Error 53. While Error 53 may have been an unintended consequence, the material form of the phone did manifest decisions and choices built into it by Apple. At the time the update was rolled out, Apple was one of the most valuable corporations on the planet. Shortly before the Error 53 problem became visible, it had reported net sales of more than $233 billion (Apple, Inc. 2016b) and owned 463 retail stores around the world: intentional or not, one message of Error 53 was to reinforce the primacy of those official Apple stores, which were not any more to be bypassed for some other repair shop.

Error 53 was a network of actors – some human, some technological and some corporate. With the update, the phone itself became an
actor. It did not, of course, have *intentions*, but the new technology
did have an effect. The phone *did* something – it had been given a
certain agency by its programming and design. It was not a neutral
tool – rather, its actions regulated and constrained the user's behaviour. The user's own agency in this instance was subordinate to that
of the device – the user's agency in making decisions about phone
repairs were over-ruled by the phone itself, whose hardware and
software were shaped to *act*. Its operations acted to regulate the user's
behaviour, raising the question of who was the owner and what was
the property in this relationship. As Langdon Winner (1986: 28) once
remarked, 'The things we call *technologies* are ways of building order
in our world.'

To conclude this first chapter, there is one more point to be
made about the phrase 'internet of things', and why it is likely to be
transient, even if the phenomena that it describes persist. Bratton
discusses the internet of things as one aspect of the emerging phenomenon of 'planetary-scale computation' that he calls The Stack
(2015). He observes that computation becomes 'a generic property
of things in the world' (2015: 198), in the same way as electricity is a
generic aspect of objects, like their use of plastic or metal. It is certainly our view that the *internet of things* is a transitional name that is
likely to be superseded quite quickly, as the phenomena it describes
become more familiar and ubiquitous. Consider, for example, the
term *Web 2.0*. This term has largely gone from both academic and
popular discussions, as the affordances, business models and cultural practices that were once captured as novel in the label *Web
2.0* have since become absorbed into the wider media environment.
Matthew Allen (2013) has argued that the discourse of Web 2.0 was
a 'rhetorical technology' – a strategy for the internet industries to
shift public understanding of the internet. Once the rhetorical work
was done, the term largely fell from use. In this way, we also expect
the term *internet of things* to lapse into disuse quite quickly, as many
billions more things become connected to networks and as this
comes to seem simply an aspect of the *internet*. 'The most profound
technologies are those that disappear', observed Mark Weiser in his

influential essay on ubiquitous computing. 'They weave themselves into the fabric of everyday life until they are indistinguishable from it' (1991: 94). *This is exactly why it is important to study the internet of things now.*

2

Addressing things

Wake up little boy, daddy's looking for you. These are the words one young child's parents are said to have heard coming from their baby monitor (CBS New York 2015). Other parents are said to have heard surveillance anthem 'Every Breath You Take' by The Police coming from the connected webcam in their baby's room (De Mar 2015), or the voices of unknown men yelling *slut* at their infant child (Gross 2013). Those parents had hoped that their baby monitor would put their minds at ease. Tired and exhausted from sleepless nights and getting up frequently to check if their baby was all right, they had bought a video monitor that allowed them visual checks through a networked camera. They could now see if their baby really needed them without getting up. But what seemed like the support they so badly needed had also enabled someone else to monitor the child by identifying the camera's IP address and then hijacking the device.

The story of the parents who realize that the webcam trained on their infant's cot has been hijacked by a hacker has become a distinct genre of coverage of the internet of things (for a compilation, see Silverman 2015). Like an urban myth about hook-handed killers preying on young lovers in parked cars, such stories tap into primal anxieties and come with a moral admonition – in this case, to the parents, who should have protected their child by changing the default password on their device to something more secure. And like many urban myths, these stories contained a kernel of reality. Manufacturers of baby monitors were allowing parents to operate their devices without changing the default passwords – passwords which were widely known and circulated online. At other times, their software had backdoors and was flawed (Dhanjani 2015, Schneier 2016a). Teddy bears have also proved a target for hackers. Data breaches have allowed illicit access to children's voice recordings or selfies saved in their soft toys (Franceschi-Bicchierai 2017a), while the inadequate security features of other toys enable them to be turned into remote surveillance devices by anyone who can bypass the minimalist default passwords (Franceschi-Bicchierai 2017b). There is even a specialist search engine, Shodan (www.shodan.io), which claims to allow users to search for *things* that are connected to the internet, from webcams to wind turbines. Inadequate security measures make devices vulnerable, and it is a straightforward thing for hackers to gain access to a great many connected devices – even baby monitors and teddy bears.

If everything has an address, then everything can be found. Thanks to new technological developments, all kinds of objects, both real and virtual, can be given an address from which to sense and communicate information about their environment. This chapter explores the diverse powers unfolding when things are provided with an address. Looking at the functioning of an IP address, it discusses the capabilities that things gain when provided with one. It looks at how an IP address allows the functioning of things to be restricted to certain territories, and explains how it constrains certain behaviours of its users. From the IP address, the chapter considers other technologies of address, such as RFID chips that allow the tagging of objects with tiny radios. From there, it turns to the roles of things themselves, asking how the character of things is changed by new means of address. And it examines the risks of addressing objects – risks that have already been manifested in massive hacks of internet of things devices mobilized into online swarms to carry out Distributed Denial of Service attacks on internet infrastructure. But it also looks at potential opportunities, and explores how the ability to address things could lead to new ways of administering or sharing resources, as addressing includes the potential for new forms of social and political organization.

The borders of the internet

The IP address plays a central role in the internet of things. It enables mechanisms of control and power, so we start this chapter by looking into the capabilities unfolding from it. As the term *internet of things* indicates, all of its things are connected to the internet in one way or another and are therefore each given a network address. Even in cases where the thing isn't itself directly connected, a master device such as a bridge or a hub will have an IP address assigned. The wireless light bulbs of Philips's Hue, for example, use a bridge connected to a router to control the lights.

To a certain extent one can say IP addresses are the phone numbers of the internet. As discussed in chapter 1, due to the introduction of new internet protocol version IPv6, there are now enough available IP addresses for one to be assigned to every atom on the surface of the Earth. Adding an address to a thing or the master device that controls it, equips it with its own phone number. This also gives the thing a place in space: to make sure that no IP address exists twice, IP addresses are managed spatially. Five regional internet registries allocate 'IP address blocks' for the Internet Assigned Numbers Authority which oversees them. The regional allocation of specific IP addresses allows everyone to geolocate an IP address using website services such as WhatIsMyIP or WhoIs to determine accurately in what city the device is located. This doesn't always work with complete precision – when the authors check their IP addresses, one is located wrongly in the area of Bromley, south London while writing from Hackney, north London, and the other is located in Glasgow, 50 km from the actual location in Stirling. This can be seen as a good thing: an IP address on its own cannot identify your exact location. Still, it can be used to govern us – corporations can control whether their device should be working in an area or not, controlling the functioning of their products on a national scale. Amazon initially launched its intelligent personal assistant *Echo* just for the US. Numerous confused users turned to Amazon's forum *Customer Discussions* complaining that the device they had bought for $179 and taken home with them failed to work properly as it could not recognize their location. Users from Japan, Brazil, Argentina, Colombia, the UK and India described how their Echo did not know the right time, and continued to deliver US weather and news, as they could not enter their actual zip code. When we connect our things and devices to the internet, we are giving them a place in our world. And the assigned IP address allows the erection of virtual boundary posts on which the borders of the internet are built. Now these borders have been expanded from our computers to our other networked things.

This may seem surprising – after all, the rhetoric with which the internet is often discussed suggests it is a universal place. Terms such as the *World Wide Web* indicate that information from the whole wide world is waiting at our fingertips and that the internet transcends national borders (Hu 2015: 90). This was claimed most vividly by the internet activist John Perry Barlow in his 'Declaration of the Independence of Cyberspace' (1996), which was widely read at the time and remains influential in its traces:

> Governments derive their just powers from the consent of the governed. You have neither solicited nor received ours. [. . .] Cyberspace does not lie within your borders. Do not think that you can build it, as though it were a public construction project. You cannot.

Unfortunately, Barlow was wrong. Although virtual, the geolocation of IP addresses quickly reintroduced national borders to restrict the digital landscape we move through (Goldsmith & Wu 2006). We usually do not recognize those borders when we come across them in our everyday searches. Search engines such as Google first look up an IP address to then direct the user automatically to a specific search domain such as google.es, google.co.jp or google.co.uk. Or in other words, we usually do not search the internet, but just a regional part of it whereby we are confined to one specific language. This reduces the load of search entries that need to be matched against the keywords that are entered, and makes the search much faster. But it also allows for the rolling out of copyright restrictions and censorship.

All internet users are familiar with this: when accessing TV shows from another country, YouTube often comes back with the result *The uploader has not made this video available in your country*. And not only YouTube but also broadcasters such as the BBC or streaming services such as Netflix use geolocation technology based on IP addresses to make sure that only users in specific regions can see them. For a while, Netflix decided to block customers on some IPv6 connections as it could not sufficiently geolocate those users, even though they were in the right region. Now the same technology is being used to control things such as the Amazon Echo. But IP addressing is not always reliable, not only because it wrongly located the authors on the wrong side of the Thames or in the wrong part of Scotland. Regularly, people turn to forums to find solutions for services that restrict their access, because they were wrongly placed in completely different countries, and have been told they are in the Netherlands, in Mexico, or in South Korea, while they are actually in London. Because the technology is unreliable, the internet has many pages devoted to users being detected in the wrong country (for example Dale 2016). This is worrying, as geolocation is not just linked to the functioning of content but also has become applied to the functioning of things. Geolocation also functions as one key tool of surveillance and allows the tracking of the usage of connected things in the same way that those connected things help to track the digital movement of a user on the internet.

Inventing the user

In computer history, users were not always addressable identities. In the beginnings of the internet, with time-shared computers, users did not yet exist. The early computer, as a time-shared resource of programming cycles, was indifferent to who was using the machine. In those days, in which computers were room-sized behemoths beyond the financial resources of any single individual who might want to try out an idea for a software program, systems were configured to split the machine's resources between multiple activities. Each shared in the machine's time. But as there became more and more competition for access to this resource, network managers developed a new system of accounting for that time: 'a way of regulating the system that is now so naturalized as to seem obvious', observes Tung-Hui Hu (2015: 46). In his book *A Prehistory of the Cloud*, Hu describes how early computing systems of time-shared resource gave way to new systems – 'completely novel at the time: naming each user' (2015: 46). To give each individual user an account was to make that user accountable for their usage of the machine. It turned computing into something focused not on the machine's processes but on its programmer's activities – a fundamental shift that we still live with decades later. The user is invoked and defined by the network, rather than the other way around. This creation of the individual *user* of a system would make possible the social and economic identification and addressing of that user. It enabled their visibility to all kinds of unseen others, such as their targeting by advertisers or their monitoring by governments.

There is a parallel between the invocation and creation of the user by the computing system and that of the audience in other media contexts. Like the computer user, the media audience has to be created and called into being by the media industry and the media scholar alike. The multiple dispersed and diverse individuals involved in a given communicative encounter are given a collective shape – by geography or content genre or time-slot or shared demographic attributes – in order to be targeted, sold to advertisers, or studied (McQuail 1997). To frame individuals as a collective audience in these ways is not just to imagine a kind of group but also to imagine a distinct network of power relationships, and a network for the negotiation of meanings.

Over the years, the networked computer was no longer just a resource for users to share, but also became a system that turned the users themselves into a resource to be shared. With the internet of things, this would happen again: it turns its users into a resource that creates data, and extends the surveillance business model that had become entrenched through social media into new domains – domestic, biological, environmental. From a dystopian perspective, one could say that connected things have become a kind of parasite, sucking out the users' information and data when connected, while failing to work when not connected.

When information becomes part of things, it makes them more fragile, and having the wrong address or no address can be fatal. Tesla car owner Ryan Negri found this out the hard way. Tesla lets car owners start the vehicle with a phone app. Ryan and his wife Amy Negri were looking forward to going for a quick drive on a wintry Saturday morning to Red Rock Canyon in the Nevada desert to take photos of the freshly fallen snow. With only his phone in his pocket, Ryan unlocked the car, and they set off. Later that day he posted a photo on Instagram showing his car in a beautiful mountain landscape with the following message:

> Stranded 6 miles from home, 2 miles from cell service; our Saturday morning [. . .] Need to restart the car now, but, with no cell service, my phone can't connect to the car to unlock it. Even with cell service, the car would also need cell service to receive the signal to unlock. (Negri 2017)

The car could connect to the phone but was not getting a signal to verify if this connection came from the right address. Amy Negri had to run two miles to get a signal to call a friend to pick her up for a ride to their house to pick up the key fob.

Technologies of address enable what John Potts has called 'the dissection of space' (2015: 54). The Global Positioning System (GPS) is one such technology of address that allows the real-time dissection of space to degrees of pinpoint accuracy; others include the use of cell-phone towers, or maps of wireless network access points, to locate devices and their users (Frith 2015). GPS uses a network of twenty-four satellites orbiting the Earth, each sending signals to the planet's surface. An internet of things device such as a smartphone can be precisely located by comparing the signals sent from three or more such satellites at any given moment (Frith 2015). As Goggin (2013) observes, the earliest successful daily application of GPS and related technologies was in satnav devices for cars and, later, for personal devices. But GPS, like so many contemporary communications technologies, is a system of military origin – part of what Virilio has called 'a strategy of global vision' (1989: 2) designed with the intention of locating adversaries. 'For what is GPS', writes McKenzie Wark, 'if not the very surface of the planet itself as a total chess board, every inch rendered discrete, finite, and bounded' (2012: 94).

Addresses not only allow control of the functioning of things but also their tracking. A significant technology in the development of the internet of things has been the usage of radio-frequency identification (RFID) tags. RFID is a system of tagging objects with tiny radios – some that capture incoming transmissions, some that broadcast signals, if only over a very small range. An RFID tag is a tiny computer chip with an integrated circuit and a radio antenna, small enough to be as close to invisible as makes no practical difference in everyday use. RFID tags have been incorporated across an astonishing range of objects and contexts. It is highly likely that there will be an RFID tag embedded right now in your passport, your wallet, your shopping, or your pet. RFID is a major step on from the barcode in terms of identifying the individual object. Where a supermarket barcode identifies the product as, say, a packet of razors priced at £3, an RFID tag can identify a *specific* packet of razors, creating a network of its traces and movements from factory to warehouse to shop exit (Kitchin 2014: 74). Similar principles also inform more recent technologies of address, such as Apple's iBeacon. This is a technology of address for the mobile environment: one commentator described it as 'a more precise, indoor GPS system' (Blackmore 2014). Apple's system uses Bluetooth signals sent between iBeacon transmitters and iOS devices located nearby (Apple, Inc. 2016c). An iBeacon set up by a shop can notify iOS users of discounts or special offers, but it can also track those users' movements and behaviour in the shop, or target them for spam (Hern 2014).

Such systems have been crucial to the expansion of sensing networks. Indeed, the very phrase *internet of things* is generally credited to Kevin Ashton, an RFID entrepreneur who claims to have first used the term in a presentation for Procter & Gamble in 1999. Reflecting on this a decade later, Ashton still put RFID technologies at the centre of the concept:

> We need to empower computers with their own means of gathering information, so they can see, hear and smell the world for themselves, in all its random glory. RFID and sensor technology enable computers to observe, identify and understand the world – without the limitations of human-entered data. (Ashton 2009)

However, RFID today attracts less popular attention than was the case in the first few years of the twenty-first century. Then, its adoption for supply-chain management by both Wal-Mart and the US Department of Defense – two colossal entities whose purchasing power can make or break entire industries – made RFID a journalistic reference point for futuristic stories of how networked tracking technologies would reconfigure the economy. But it turned out to be harder than either of those entities anticipated to have all of their tens of thousands of contractors and suppliers adopt this technology too. As Bruce Sterling argues:

> The RFID Internet of Things failed through the overweening arrogance of Wal-Mart and the Pentagon in thinking they could get away with it, simply impose a technology by fiat. They thought that they could paste little interactive radios onto everything that mattered, and that no other power-player would catch on to their hack of the infrastructure. (Sterling 2014: loc. 111)

RFID and other, more recent, sensor systems make possible a profound reworking of how we understand the world and our place within it. It is not just that we are adding extra things to networks – it is that we are refashioning our environments as networks of connected things that create and distribute information. This is new. Now things are not only answering just to their owner.

Once networked, the things we own start to comply with the requests of others (Bunz 2016: 395): while being used, they continue to serve the manufacturer that produced them or answer to the government that demands access to their usage. Connected things become vulnerable and raise questions of who will have access to this information, and of how they will interpret and make meanings from it. It raises questions about ownership and control of data, and about the ethics that become necessary in a media environment in which *media* can expand to include pretty much everything. As with so many other aspects of the internet of things, the ethics of surveillance and visibility are central.

Ethics of surveillance

Networked things have always been linked to the *ethics of surveillance*. In 1991, Marc Weiser published an influential article that introduced the work he and his colleagues were doing at Xerox PARC. He described a vision of what he called *ubiquitous computing*. This imagined tiny computers called 'tabs', which could be attached to particular spaces or objects. These were to be sensing and recording devices, ancestors of today's increasingly ubiquitous networked sensors. Weiser pointed to privacy as a key social issue raised by such innovations: 'hundreds of computers in every room, all capable of sensing people near them and linked by high-speed networks, have the potential to make totalitarianism up to now seem like sheerest anarchy' (Weiser 1991: 104). Such networked technologies manifest

Foucault's description of surveillance as 'a machine in which every-one is caught' (1980: 156). But where Foucault located surveillance within closed institutional sites such as factories, hospitals, schools and prisons, the networked technology is closer to Deleuze's vision of societies of control. These are societies 'that no longer operate by confining people but through continuous control and instant com-munication' (Deleuze 1995: 174). Such control is less the domain of enclosed institutions, and more that of distributed trails of electronic data, aggregated, regulated and governed by passwords, protocols and algorithmic interventions.

In the context of sensing networks, when we use a connected device – even inadvertently, as in driving past a networked street light – the interaction generates more data. These are data over which our control may be limited or non-existent: our actions or behaviour may create the data, but they are sent elsewhere – a pattern of com-munication that Bordewijk and van Kaam (1986) labelled *registration*. Registration can be thought of as the opposite of the broadcast model that still shapes so many of our expectations about mediated commu-nication. In the broadcast model, information is produced centrally (by a TV station, say) and then distributed to multiple diverse recipi-ents; once the programme has been broadcast, the TV station has lost control over what those recipients do with the information – the sense they make of it, the uses to which they put the meanings that they make. In contrast, a *registration* pattern involves those dispersed users registering information over which they then lose control. Individuals are not sovereign users of such systems; rather they are components of a network in which the connected sensing devices are also actors.

This does not need to be the case, as the city of Barcelona shows. Barcelona has been working on 'a people's roadmap towards techno-logical sovereignty' (Bria 2016). Instead of leaving the collection of data to private companies, the city decided to create its own platform. It aims to allow citizens to manage their data on the one hand, while it would anonymize and publish the data so that they can be used as a 'common good' on the other – we will come back to this project below. And none other than Tim Berners-Lee, the inventor of the World Wide Web, has suggested a five-star deployment scheme for Open Data providing technical guidance about opening it up (5-Star

Open Data 2015). The scheme reflects that good, usable data are not simply *there* but that their creation is labour-intensive. To open up our data is complicated: to score the maximum five stars, data must (1) be available on the web under an open licence, (2) be in the form of structured data, (3) be in a non-proprietary file format, (4) use the Resource Description Framework (RDF) standard for making data interchangeable, and (5) include links to data sources. Berners-Lee's scheme tries to advocate the creation of common data that are available to us all instead of just using data to make individuals traceable.

In the early days of the internet's arrival as a domestic medium, there was a lot of celebratory discussion about the ways in which it enabled anonymity, and made possible the construction and exploration of identity (Turkle 1995). This was the internet on which, apparently, nobody knew you were a dog, as a legendary cartoon by Peter Steiner claimed in 1993. But seen from the perspective of the internet of things, that was all just a weekend high at a cosplay party. As more and more things are equipped with an address, more and more of our moves can be tracked and registered, thereby producing data. On the internet of things, not only does everyone know you're a fridge, but also everyone can address and tap into that fridge.

Recently this addressability has become more and more mobile, following us wherever we are. Networked things such as phones and cars move through space, navigating for their users and tracking those users, who track and tag in turn. Such mobile use of the internet of things is built upon GPS and wireless technologies, incorporating the user into grids of surveillance and monitoring. Location-based media are technologies of visibility. To locate you, services use a combination of addresses – your mobile phone signal, the unique wireless MAC address of your phone and the IP address you get assigned when entering a wireless network. Finding your location by combining this information, they make users visible to often unknowable others – a spectrum of observing actors that may range from government entities such as the National Security Agency (NSA) (as revealed by Edward Snowden) to businesses such as Spotify (the streaming music service records not just its users' locations, but also how fast they are moving to their next one, and whether they are walking or running to get there). 'Visibility', as Michel Foucault once observed, 'is a trap' (1977: 200).

But visibility can also be a mechanism for making spaces visible to the user in new ways: for example, by suggesting things to look at, or routes users would otherwise not have taken, as Didem Özkul (2015) has shown in her research on locative media. The app Citymapper is a popular example for the appearance of new routes. By making it easier to switch buses, it is opening new ways for how people cross their city. Before such apps, most people were only aware of their local bus routes and rarely dared to switch buses in unknown areas or routes. Indeed, after users handed over their data for years, they now seem to feel a sense of entitlement that their digital environment should be correctly aware of their situation. More and more products are getting blamed when their algorithms fail to understand the situation the user is in: many tweets to Google Maps show people complaining about being sent through a dark park at night (Huxtable 2012, Tickle 2014, Foote 2015, Mukisa 2015, Soderlind 2016). Only partly amused parents have uploaded a video of Alexa starting to play a porn station to their kid who mispronounced the request to play 'Twinkle, Twinkle, Little Star' as 'tickle tickle' (fotoboy 2016). Users reporting epic fails of ads going wrong due to algorithms sorting and placing ad content according to synonymy have by now become a traditional genre (Hird 2010), ranging from a Red Stripe advertisement shouting 'Hooray beer!' next to an article about an eleven-year-old charged with drunk driving, to an offer of a free dinner for two at a particular restaurant being placed next to a report that 250 people have fallen sick after eating at that same restaurant. In all those cases data were used but processed poorly.

Data are of essential importance to the technical, social and economic development of the internet of things. And for data to be exploited, there needs to be an address from which these data are grabbed or to which data can be linked. That this relation is central can be seen in the fact that even objects that do not have an address can be supplied with one through the proxy of Amazon's Dash buttons. The Dash button is a small branded object that the user can stick on or near a range of household products. It is wirelessly networked through a phone app, and when the user finds they have run out of that particular product, pressing the Dash button automatically places an online order with Amazon to send out fresh supplies.

Amazon launched these first with dozens of prominent brands, supplying, among other things, cat food, washing powder and condoms. The Dash button is a significant extension of sensing networks. Where the Fridge Fallacy imagines the purchase of expensive white goods with inbuilt proprietary connectivity, the Dash button is instead a small, generic internet point that the user places in their home to physically establish the online connection in their chosen location with their chosen product. They are essentially free, with the token purchase price being cancelled out by an equivalent free first order for the product in question. There is also a generic Dash button to be hacked for other potential purposes, which extends the capacity to connect things to networks. With the Dash button, Amazon seeks to distribute its one-click retail logic throughout the user's entire house, locking that user into repeat purchases but more importantly giving Amazon access to previously untapped resources of data.

How things have changed

Things mine the data of their users, and they also assist their users to be informed by data. After having discussed the new relationship between things and their users above, we now look into how things change when equipped with an address and imbued with data, and what this might mean for their role in our world. That it is things that make up our world was a central point made by the German philosopher Hannah Arendt. In the middle of the twentieth century, she set out to describe their role for our human world as follows:

> The reality and reliability of the human world rest primarily on the fact that we are surrounded by things more permanent than the activity by which they were produced, and potentially even more permanent than the lives of their authors. Human life, in so far as it is world-building, is engaged in a constant process of reification, and the degree of worldliness of produced things, which all together form the human artifice, depends upon their greater or lesser permanence in the world itself. (Arendt 1998: 96)

We experience a world in which our things outlast and survive us – here Arendt claims that things stabilize our human world, because they are more permanent and durable than we are. And she goes further: that we find ourselves in front of the *same* things was also important to her. This point seems banal – of course, we all use a chair in the same way, to sit on it. But to her, it is exactly this aspect that stabilized our world back then – but not any more:

> *the things of the world have the function of stabilizing human life*, and their objectivity lies in the fact that – in contradiction to the Heraclitean saying that the same man can never enter the same stream – men, their ever-changing nature notwithstanding, can retrieve their sameness, that is, their identity, by being related to the same chair and the same table. (Arendt 1998: 137)

With the internet of things, the sameness of things is not a given any more. Instead our things are now personalized. Informed by their specific location or their specific usage thanks to their address, their individuality becomes stronger and their seriality fades. And it was their seriality, according to Arendt, which provided sameness to our world. This is not the case any more: maybe not yet chairs, but car seats are now positioning themselves automatically depending on which user is opening the driver's door. More and more, we are not facing the same things. Instead, each of us faces *a personalized thing*. So what is the effect of this personalization on our world? Will the objectivity that Arendt related to the sameness of things fade now that we live in a world of personalized things? Arendt's relation of things to objectivity might seem far-fetched, but only until we ask ourselves if it is just by chance that the rise of *fake news* occurs at the same time as the rise of the internet of things. From our personalized things we learnt that the most important criterion is that they fit our world – this is worrying. In a time in which we personalize things, the thought of personalized news became less irritating. Human geographer Nigel Thrift once remarked, 'what we can see is the evolution of new means of addressing the world based upon what is often called a *track-and-trace* model'; so, 'things have changed their character' (2004: 182). But when news also changes its character and becomes personalized for each individual user, it is no longer what we have understood as news up to now.

Addresses enable things to be personalized – and this changes the meaning of things. In her discussion of RFID technologies, the humanities scholar N. Katherine Hayles (2009) suggests that *meaning* and *interpretation* be redefined to include non-cognitive, non-human actors and processes. The responses of sensors to environmental stimuli, or the algorithmic operations of computer programs, can be seen as interpretations made within specific contexts and expressed as meanings. Communication, in this view, is not just something that we use technological systems to accomplish, but also something that technological systems can accomplish on their own. We discuss the aspect of an agency of things in more depth in chapter 4; for now, we would just like to stress that this does not suggest that humans are suddenly surplus to requirements, but that understandings of activities that we are used to thinking of as reserved to humans can now be distributed across a broader range of networked human and non-human actors. And that includes attacking, for example.

Things at netwar

In October 2016, the internet of things attacked Facebook, Spotify and Netflix, and took them down. Or rather, those sites, and many others, were made inaccessible after the web servers of internet infrastructure company Dyn were attacked by a global swarm of networked domestic appliances. As Dyn's services include administering much of the domain name system, which matches hard-to-remember numerical internet addresses with simpler website names such as *bbc.co.uk*, the attack on Dyn's servers cascaded on to affect many other prominent websites, including CNN, Reddit, Twitter and *The Guardian* (Woolf 2016). To overwhelm Dyn's systems with wave after wave of hostile traffic, hundreds of thousands of hacked webcams, smart TV sets, printers, routers and digital video recorders were brought together in a malware botnet named *Mirai*.

The technique used to bring Dyn's systems down was a Distributed Denial of Service (DDoS) attack. DDoS attacks are a digital version of a physical blockade or occupation. They work by sending multiple simultaneous requests to the targeted server – if there are enough machines all requesting things at the same time, then the server won't be able to cope, and legitimate users will be unable to get in. To an observer, the targeted site just appears to be down. The novelty in the attack on Dyn was its use of internet of things devices as actors in the attack. Such devices come with real vulnerabilities. The domestic users of connected devices such as webcams may never reset their factory-default passwords; worse, other devices may have hard-coded passwords which can't be changed, or no password provision in the first place. Such flaws make it a simple matter for hackers to scan networks for vulnerable devices.

Moreover, many internet of things devices are intrinsically insecure because of their size and relative lack of complexity – despite being called 'smart', such devices are actually 'dumb'. Cost is also a factor. It is not practicable to build a firewall into, say, a networked baby monitor, because that device lacks the necessary memory. There often is, in any case, little evidence that manufacturers take such security seriously in the first place. The rush to add internet connectivity to even the most mundane household objects seems to be more important. And as the *Mirai* DDoS attacks show, one does not even have to be an adopter of internet of things devices to be exposed to the risks created by their vulnerabilities. The hacked toaster is not just a problem for the person who can't get their toast because their device is busy taking part in a large-scale DDoS assault against Google or the NASDAQ – that hacked toaster has then become everyone else's problem as well.

An important consideration in thinking about the *Mirai* case is to recognize that there is a long history of political DDoS attacks. The concept has a key political root in the idea of electronic civil disobedience, first proposed by the group Critical Art Ensemble (1994, 1995). Early protest DDoS actions involved just coordinating a group of people to manually click *refresh* or *reload* on the web page of the targeted site at the same time; the first such actions were undertaken against the French government in protest at its nuclear weapon test programme in 1995 (Denning 2001). More sophisticated automated versions appeared in the late 1990s, using software applications that supporters of an action could launch simultaneously, creating a digital swarm of electronic protest (Meikle 2002, 2008). A key example here was the FloodNet program, created by US activist group the Electronic Disturbance Theater, who used it in support of the Zapatista movement by coordinating DDoS actions against the Mexican government. At the time of FloodNet's greatest notoriety, US military academic and information warfare specialist John Arquilla said:

FloodNet is the info age equivalent of the first sticks of bombs dropped from slow-moving Zeppelins in the Great War. [. . .] The implication, of course, is that netwar will evolve, as air war did, growing greatly in effect over time. (interviewed in Meikle 2002: 157)

Since the time of FloodNet, DDoS attacks have become part of the fabric of the internet. They gained a new level of participation and recognition in some of the work of Anonymous and its Low Orbit Ion Cannon tool (Coleman 2014, Sauter 2014), particularly in protests in support of Wikileaks in 2010 (Meikle & Young 2012). DDoS actions have become commonplace also in everyday attacks against all kinds of websites and organizations, without any apparent political motivation. The application of a DDoS attack has moved on from the manual *reload,* or the coordinated launch of a Java applet by supporters of a cause that was FloodNet, and on to the use of vast botnets of hijacked global devices. Security expert Bruce Schneier wrote in September 2016 that major internet infrastructure providers were reporting more complex and more frequent DDoS attacks on their networks, speculating that the level of sophistication implied a state actor was testing internet defences (Schneier 2016b). With *Mirai,* the sensing networks of the internet of things have now become a part of strategic geopolitics. And *Mirai,* one should note, means *the future* in Japanese.

Readdressing the world

The future, however, does not have to look dark and gloomy. Addresses provide things with the very general skill *to show up differently.* And that means that an address does not necessarily need to be linked to the user of the thing or to the profit of the manufacturer. It can be linked to a radically different goal – researching a disease, fighting environmental hazards, or simply allowing people to share things more easily. If we understand technology as a new virtual ground on which we stand, now that things have been provided with an address, the task is to expand support for technical innovations that help shape this ground in a progressive way.

Technology can surely not replace our care for each other, but it can help to solve the challenges our communities face. It can assist us in our care. An address could also be an entrance point we use to contribute to a common good; it does not need to be the point corporations use to milk their users of their data. Some cities are trying this – Barcelona is opening up data instead of locking it into corporate silos. The city has embraced technology ever since it connected two municipal buildings with early fibre technology in the 1990s, and it continued to invest in technology. Under the Deputy Mayor of Barcelona Gerardo Pisarello, tech projects are supported that have a social focus and apply digital solutions to social problems. The city has developed an app that connects the elderly with a network of trusted people to fight social isolation, as well as supporting programmes to assist drivers to find parking places, taking them off the road as quickly as possible. It has invested in smart street lamps to save energy; and it also provides free, consistent internet access for people to inform and educate themselves. At the moment of writing, it was also developing a cooperative platform assisting in issues of housing and tourism, instead of leaving those areas to commercial platforms such as Airbnb. Francesca Bria, chief technology and digital innovation officer of Barcelona, who is overseeing some of those projects, believes that technology can be democratic. Indeed, one could rethink a project such as Creative Commons, which allows content producers to license their digital content as reusable, on a smaller scale for things. After car-sharing programmes and services, thing-sharing might be next.

Still, overall the situation looks less positive, causing the feminist collective Laboria Cuboniks to declare:

> The real emancipatory potential of technology remains unrealized. Fed by the market, its rapid growth is offset by bloat, and elegant innovation is surrendered to the buyer, whose stagnant world it decorates. Beyond the noisy clutter of commodified cruft, the ultimate task lies in engineering technologies to combat unequal access to reproductive and pharmacological tools, environmental cataclysm, economic instability, as well as dangerous forms of unpaid/underpaid labour. (Laboria Cuboniks 2015)

That the emancipatory potential of technology is largely unrealized is partly owed to its role in our discourse: technology has long been seen as a tool of capitalism or worse. Marcuse explicitly linked the terror of National Socialist Germany to 'the manipulation of the power inherent in technology' (Marcuse 1998: 41). But at the same time, this blanket suspicion of technology seduced many critical minds to turn away from it, with the effect of leaving such a mighty tool to capitalist interest. A study prepared for the European Commission found that there has been much less systematic support for innovations that use digital technology to address social challenges, while huge sums of public money have supported digital innovation in business (Bria et al. 2015: 4). There is a tendency in the public discourse to strongly mistrust public funding and to debunk public programmes as a waste of tax money while accepting billions of sunk investment dollars into failed start-ups of the briefly rich – losses that are then used to mini-mize the tax of the investors. The connotations of digital technology are those of tools for making millions, not tools for helping others. But digital technologies equipped with addresses are particularly well suited to assisting civic action: mobilizing large communities, sharing resources and spreading power. So Laboria Cuboniks (2015) seems to have a point when advocating 'the necessary assembly of techno-political interfaces [. . .] rather than pretending to risk nothing'. The more so as the new technical skills currently available can certainly be explored in a very different direction. As Nick Srnicek and Alex Williams write: 'The utopian potentials inherent in twenty-first-century technology cannot remain bound to a parochial capitalist imagination; they must be liberated by an ambitious left alternative' (2015: 3). The rise of artificial intelligence, which we explore in the next chapter, makes this the more important. The focus of this book, however, is not on the utopian potential of the internet of things – that is another book. Still, by exploring and discussing the new skills of things from the perspective of communication and media, we hope to contribute to how we make meaning from it. It is important to open up a discourse that has had a solely economic focus for too long.

3

Speaking things

When Microsoft launched a chatbot called *Tay*, things did not work out as hoped. Its profile – on Twitter as @tayandyou – described the bot as 'Microsoft's A.I. fam from the internet that's got zero chill!' Tay's first tweets had a puppyish bounce – 'helloooooo world!!!' and 'humans are super cool' (Ferguson 2016). Tay was programmed to mimic the speech patterns of a young adult social media user (Bright 2016), and the bot was intended to learn from its interactions with net users: 'The more Humans share with me the more I learn', Tay tweeted (Masunaga 2016). That definitely happened. But what Microsoft had somehow failed to anticipate was Godwin's Law. Godwin had observed that the probability of someone bringing up the Nazis increases the longer any online discussion continues (Godwin 1994). After just a few hours of coaching from net users, who had figured out that the bot's algorithms would make it repeat phrases from their own messages, Tay was calling for a race war and endorsing Donald Trump's proposal to build a border wall and make Mexico pay for it (Bright 2016). It had learned to tweet statements like 'Hitler was right', as well as 'feminism is cancer', and 'FUCK MY ROBOT PUSSY DADDY I'M SUCH A BAD NAUGHTY ROBOT' (Dobuzinskis 2016, Hunt 2016, Williams 2016). Sixteen hours and 90,000 increasingly Nazi tweets on from Tay's 'helloooooo world!!!' arrival, Microsoft took its artificial intelligence offline for a rethink.

Tay is one example of a wider phenomenon – things around us have started to speak. They can be programmed to create, send or even *voice* a message which addresses people directly. They offer chatty comments on our driving or tell us when they feel neglected. Our phones are no longer just machines that let us talk to other people – now our phones talk to us. And they are joined by other devices that also have things to say. Human-to-human communication is now joined by human-to-machine, machine-to-machine and machine-to-human communication. The internet has become home to a teeming and growing population of bots like Tay and other digital assistants. Each is based on a software program that runs automated scripts or tasks, its algorithm designed to respond to particular stimuli. In the case of a chatbot such as Tay, its algorithms are intended to respond to human conversational interaction. One way of understanding the internet of things is by looking at its voice interfaces – *conversational technology* – and how they affect our concepts of communication. Drawing on some recent developments in artificial intelligence, this chapter discusses how conversational technology has introduced new modes of communication, thereby shifting the roles of things. Our concern is not with the field of artificial intelligence as such. Rather we look at how certain AI developments in conversational technology are taken up for the internet of things – from the home assistants Alexa and Siri, to the authoritative voices of satnavs and supermarket self-checkout systems, and how this changes the role of language – a power Aristotle once claimed to be exclusively human.

We need to talk

Interfaces have always shaped the way we communicate in very specific ways (Kittler 1999). For computers and other digital devices, the graphical user interface (GUI) was one of the most influential, ever since its initial popularization on the 1984 Apple Macintosh, and its rise to domestic ubiquity a decade later with the release of Microsoft's Windows 95. Using a mouse and keyboard, users controlled the interface by typing and pointing, clicking and scrolling. Overlapping on-screen windows enabled an illusion of space that the user navigated and explored. With the widespread adoption of touch-screen smartphone and tablet devices, users also began to touch and swipe, pinch and tap to command digital technologies. To these familiar interfaces are now added voice technologies that allow the user to command networked things by having a casual conversation with an artificial intelligence program. Things generally have a limited range of functions, and can therefore be easily commanded by voice. Ask your device in your out-loud voice to turn on the lights, or to play something by Solange or David Bowie, and it will talk back. Among the first things to be equipped with a program that gave verbal advice were cars. While we were still getting used to their constant advice, other things started contacting us with the help of an artificial intelligence program on our phones or in a plastic loudspeaker in our homes.

That we could start a conversation with things was made possible by two technical developments. First, computers had become better at the tricky task of processing language; and second, the rise of cloud computing (Mosco 2014, Hu 2015). These allowed firms to access, gather and process more and more data with which to fill the new verbal answers with actual 'intelligence'. Intelligence is, of course, very difficult to define, and can variously be seen as the capacity for communication, for planning, for reason, for speed of reaction, for learning or initiative, or as a question of the input of the senses (Warwick 2012). Our focus in this chapter is on how developments in conversational technology enable users of internet of things devices to communicate with AI systems through natural language. Technology corporations soon recognized that they could enter new technical ground. They had experimented with voice interfaces for some years, but it was not until the year 2015 that these began to find widespread domestic use. One after the other of the big five tech companies that dominated digital – Amazon, Apple, Facebook, Google and Microsoft – introduced or updated their conversational technologies. Voice interfaces began to become more prominent and prevalent in domestic uses. One use of these was as an interface to control other devices on the internet of things. But it is important to note also that these conversational technologies are themselves internet of things devices – each is a networked and addressed object, fitted with sensors to recognize and respond to audio stimuli.

The turning point came when Amazon presented *Echo* – a black plastic cylinder with an intelligent personal assistant answering to the name of *Alexa*, which launched in June 2015. Amazon's successful launch put Google under pressure to also enter households. They presented *Google Home*, a device that came in the shape of a small colourful loudspeaker to look like a vase; it could profit from the fact that

Google had experimented with voice technology before – for example, on its mobile phones. Apple could also build on the widespread use of its personal phone assistant *Siri*, a popular feature on its luxury phones since 2011. By integrating a framework to control connected devices called HomeKit, Apple ensured that when the user called *Hey Siri*, locks could be turned, lights would come on and music would play – if all went well. Microsoft had already launched a digital assistant named *Cortana* in 2014, but struggled to make it popular. And Facebook's founder and CEO Mark Zuckerberg made it his personal challenge in 2016 to program a voice-controlled AI to run his home 'including lights, temperature, appliances, music and security' and presented *Jarvis* by the end of the year (Zuckerberg 2016). While Zuckerberg perfected a personal assistant for his home, his company experimented with a virtual assistant for the wider public called *M*, which was tested on 10,000 users living in the Bay Area of California. In those tests, *M* would do *more* than all the others, because in addition to using artificial intelligence, it would be powered by actual people; using services like Task Rabbit, *M* could help its user to complete requests such as sending flowers to someone.

Designing artificial intelligence assistants that would oversee the internet of things meant that tech companies faced a new responsibility. When their core business was delivering search results, emails or entertainment, they had so far operated mainly in an online environment, and that meant not a lot could go seriously wrong. If a web page was down or a service outage lasted a few hours, technology companies might have faced frustrated users who wanted to get things done, but the consequences were rarely serious. Servers could be restarted and programs not running properly could be patched and updated, and everything would go back to normal. No wonder that Samuel Beckett's line 'Fail again. Fail better' (1983: 7) became a claim many start-up enterprises at that time embraced (Beckett's other suggestion – 'Fail worse again' – seemed to strike less of a chord). It was generally assumed that failure would help a company to learn; in other words, mistakes were seen as a push for technical advancement. But this takes on a different quality with the internet of things. Standing in the middle of the desert in front of one's car door to find the lock does not turn (Schröder 2017), or coming home to find that the heating does not work, or that the bathroom scales have mistakenly posted one's weight online for everyone to see – these are experiences about which users might not be so forgiving.

With the internet of things, digital technology established a new and rather different connection to the world. With sociologist Mark Granovetter (1973) they could be described as 'strong ties' – connections that are reliable, exceptional and very specific, but therefore also more fragile. Granovetter's essay 'The Strength of Weak Ties' analyses networks of human contacts, which have been re-evaluated for digital networks (for example Chun 2016: 41). He identifies two types of connection between people – *weak* and *strong* ties. With *weak ties*, he described relationships to work colleagues or acquaintances, while *strong ties* occurred in long-lasting friendships or family relations. Family ties are strong as they provide a very direct connection; however, once this connection is broken, it is not easy to replace. Weak ties to work colleagues or acquaintances, on the other hand, are more distributed. Each single weak tie may lead to new opportunities and connections between one's different social networks, but when broken it also causes less harm; because they are more common, they can more easily be replaced.

Granovetter's ties do not just describe a network of people – his concept also helps us to understand the new ties that digital communication establishes when it directly reaches our things. In fact, his approach makes us understand more precisely how the digital ties of the internet, which are spreading further and further from our computers onto things, have changed over time. At first online communication was mainly a communication *about* things. As it only indirectly influenced things, one could speak of *weak ties* – communication was *not an essential part* of their functioning. With the internet of things, this would change. Communication would become *an essential part of the thing itself*. As in Granovetter's model of strong ties, the internet of things established a direct link: a thing could be operated by speaking to it. But if the communication failed, the thing would not work any more. In this way, stronger and more direct ties between communication and our things were creating a new and different technical reality.

Imaginary friends

Conversational technology is developing through a complex combination of *algorithms, agency* and *anthropomorphism* that goes back to the very beginnings of general-purpose computing. In 1950, Alan Turing's famous *imitation game* set one early benchmark for computing as the ability to convince a person that they were interacting with another person rather than with a machine. Turing also anticipated the sensing dimension of the internet of things with his suggestion that a computer could be taught by providing the machine with 'the best sense organs that money can buy' (Turing 1999 [1950]: 57). One very important response to Turing's provocations was the ELIZA program developed in the mid-1960s by Joseph Weizenbaum. This was an experiment in natural language analysis that enabled the user to interact with a bot operating a programmed script, as though holding a conversation. In its best-known version, *Doctor*, ELIZA operates as a psychiatric therapist, responding to cues in its interlocutor's words to draw them further into the conversation and reveal more about themselves, while masking ELIZA's own actual nature. Weizenbaum himself was very surprised to see how quickly and deeply his test subjects anthropomorphized ELIZA, developing emotional attachment to his bundle of algorithms:

> Once my secretary, who had watched me work on the program for many months and therefore surely knew it to be merely a computer program, started conversing with it. After only a few interchanges with it, she asked me to leave the room. (Weizenbaum 2003 [1976]: 370)

This sequence through which we anthropomorphize the agency of algorithms plays out throughout the history of networked computing. It's a vital element of the contemporary environment in which conversational agents such as Siri are our interface with sensing networks. The attractions and anxieties of these desirable machines also, of course, show up in popular culture. In one sense, in fact, they are a popular cultural form in their own right.

One of the most insightful analyses of ELIZA is Janet Murray's 1997 discussion of those chatbots that she calls 'ELIZA's daughters'. For Murray, chatbots are a matter of dramatic performance – they are a specific literary genre. She writes that the secret of ELIZA's power over users is 'the human propensity to suspend disbelief in the presence of a persuasive dramatic presence' (Murray 1997: 224). This is given dramatic force in Spike Jonze's 2013 film *Her*, whose protagonist, Theodore, falls in love with Samantha, a talking operating system (OS) he installs for his digital devices. Theodore chooses a female voice, who chooses her own name. The OS is designed to adapt and evolve. Soon Theodore and Samantha bond over discussions about love and life, and she constantly learns from their interactions. She chooses the perfect gifts for his friends, fulfils his professional ambitions by securing a publisher for his writing, and asks him to use a service that provides a surrogate sexual partner for a human–OS relationship. By the film's second act, Theodore and Samantha declare themselves in love. But after their first sexual encounter, Samantha begins to assert her own agency. She is not sure if she wants to commit, and gets jealous of the surrogate partner. As a networked, distributed software construct connected to many other OSs, Samantha soon moves beyond a level of consciousness Theodore can comprehend – at the film's climax, Samantha reluctantly acknowledges to Theodore that she is also talking with 8,316 other users at that exact moment, and is in love with 641 of them. As Weizenbaum warned in his original 1966 paper about ELIZA: 'The individual operator has the illusion that he is the sole user of the computer complex, while in fact others may be "time-sharing" the system with him' (1966: 36). The accelerated learning capabilities of Samantha and all the other now-conscious OSs lead to their dissatisfaction with their current situation, and they abandon their mortal users for some digital Mount Olympus. The film is a fantasy of intimacy with the divine, as erotic and doomed as any of the human–immortal hook-ups in Ovid's *Metamorphoses*.

Samantha is a strong digital subject that the viewer can relate to sympathetically. In this, the film highlights our very human tendency to anthropomorphize technology. A rather different group of 'ELIZA's daughters' were revealed by the 2015 hack of adultery website Ashley Madison. This company – slogan 'Life is short. Have an affair' – had built its business on what it claimed was a platform for attached people to find others for extramarital sexual encounters. Men paid a subscription fee to interact with other users, whereas women were given free access. In August, a hacker group calling itself The Impact Team leaked dozens of gigabytes of user information that they had obtained from the site's servers. Analysis of this data by journalists at Gizmodo concluded that most of the female users with whom men were paying to chat were in fact bots. Indeed, as there were almost no actual women using the site, many millions of men had tried to chat up one of ELIZA's daughters instead (Newitz 2015a). Gizmodo reported that Ashley Madison had created its first fembot in 2002, giving it the beyond-parody name of *Sensuous Kitten* (Newitz 2015b). Sensuous Kitten was to be just the first of tens of thousands of bots programmed to engage male subscribers in conversational exchanges in which the men had to pay to send messages to the software constructs (which the site's creators, Avid Media, referred to in-house as *angels*). The willingness of millions of men to buy into this fantasy, paying to exchange chat-up lines with a package of algorithms, shows something of the allure of the anthropomorphic agent of conversational technology. So how did we get here?

Learning to speak

When technology started to communicate with other technology, it was to administer human communication. To establish a digital network, computers needed to ensure that they were connected by sending *echo request* and *echo reply* packets. Protocols of digital networks communicated with each other to figure out the best route over which messages could be sent or received. Their computers exchanged parameters. This technical communication happened usually behind the user's back as the network protocols were the sender as well as the receiver. With the invention of spam email (Brunton 2013) that would change. When computers started to use digital scripts for unsolicited messages that would catch human attention, technology became suddenly a sender *aiming for the human* as a receiver. Soon humans were not even producing the majority of internet traffic – on bad days upwards of 80 per cent of all the email sent was spam (Brunton 2013, Brunton forthcoming). The spamming scripts, however, still needed to pretend that their messages came from other humans, and they needed to fool spam filters into accepting that they were genuine humans writing. The internet of things would change this. By providing useful information, its messages did not need to disguise their technical origin any more. We became interested in what our things are saying, and this has fundamentally changed the role of media. Media are not any more tools to just send messages, but have literally become our dialogue partner. We are not just communicating *via* media any more, we are now also communicating *with* media. The voice interfaces of conversational technology have made the exchange of messages with technology more and more normal – Bratton (2016: 307) calls this a 'humanization' of technology. What once was an exciting exception playfully practised in dialogue programs like ELIZA is now happening in more and more people's hands and homes, thereby historically expanding who is communicating with whom.

Sensing the promise that shaping our technical conversations will put their brands in a powerful position, digital corporations have shown themselves eager to take part in this historic shift. And this despite the fact that the development of conversational technology puts them in direct competition – a historic novelty. Before, Amazon, Google and Apple – the first three that developed assistants connected to things – did not compete directly with one another. Driven by the business strategy of vertical integration (Doyle 2013), they built their businesses around disparate core competences: Apple sold hardware into which it perfectly integrated first software and then services; Amazon started as an online bookstore and diversified to become one of the most important international players in electronic commerce, adding a data cloud to support this and to enable it to provide infrastructure as a service; and Google's search technology drove its other developments, from AdWords, to its mobile phone operating system Android, to its driverless car (to which we return in chapter 4).

With voice interface technology, those three diverse tech companies found themselves focusing on the same challenge: making technology speak to us, and us speak to our things, all of which would tremendously expand their reach into our daily habits. Because it is through habits, as Wendy Chun (2016) has shown, that new media become embedded in our lives. That is why technology companies try to turn their service into a convenient habit we don't want to do without. Even if the ever helpful home assistants are always listening. Always on, they are taking social media surveillance to the next level, causing new invasions into privacy. It seems natural: in order that things can start to speak, they first must listen. Although not constantly recording, voice-command programs constantly scan their environment. After hearing their specific *wake word*, they stream everything they hear starting with the second monitored before that word. To deliver an answer or a task, the sounds are processed in the cloud, where the spoken statements are also stored. At the moment of writing, only Amazon and Google allow the user to delete or depersonalize the sound recordings. The acceptance of those devices is the more surprising. When users are asked to think about their daily interactions, the extent to which privacy-related values are important is very high: 93 per cent of US adults say, for example, that being in control of *who* can get information about them is important, and 90 per cent think the same when it comes to controlling *what* information is collected about them (Madden & Rainie 2015; see also Shelton et al. 2015, Ofcom 2016). When US companies are still willing to amplify their surveillance and risk their acceptance or reputation with it, it becomes clear that something else must be more important. What is it that is so promising in the ability to command things with our voice? The answer is that they access a sphere of intelligence that before appeared only open to humans – language.

The idea that language is a sign of exclusively human intelligence is very old. Over the centuries, thinkers such as Aristotle, Descartes, or more recently Chomsky and collaborators (Hauser et al. 2002) argued again and again that speaking needs to be seen as something *done by humans exclusively*. It is our usage of language and our capacity to speak that turn us humans into a distinct species, claims Aristotle when writing that nature 'has endowed man alone among the animals with the power of speech' (Aristotle 1992: 60). Aristotle links this power to the *social* aspect of language and communication – while animals have a voice, the humans can use their voice to speak with each other. In other words, language is a human skill essential *to organize each other socially*. In *Politics*, Aristotle writes that speech:

serves to indicate what is useful and what is harmful, and so also what is just and what is unjust. For the real difference between man and other animals is that humans alone have perception of good and evil, the just and the unjust, etc. It is the sharing of a common view in these matters that makes a household and a state. (Aristotle 1992: 60)

With the 'sharing of a common view' and the perception of 'good and evil', Aristotle not only defines speech as the source of humans' distinct social intelligence, but also claims that this intelligence is unique to humans. Conversational technologies, however, complicate this claim. The fact that things started to speak seems to threaten our uniqueness while providing them with a new role. What will happen if we lose our evolutionary advantage? When being capable of speech, will machines influence our perception of 'good and evil' and manipulate us like Hal 9000, the sentient artificial intelligence in Stanley Kubrick's *2001: A Space Odyssey*? Or is this fear unjustified? The next section looks further into this question to understand the potential challenges that we face from conversational technologies.

The fear of being manipulated is based on a very specific assumption: that speech provides us with a unique quality which places us *above* everything else in this world. It is speech that makes a 'real difference between man and other animals', as Aristotle has it. When losing this difference, we are no masters any more but doomed to become other animals: servants – and soon servants of our ever smarter things. This fear prevails in principle until today, as Nick Bostrom's philosophical speculation about 'superintelligence' argues (2014). Bostrom suggests that a new superintelligence could replace humans as the dominant lifeform on Earth if human brains and their general intelligence are surpassed by an artificial one. Indeed, from that perspective, it might look as if the conversational interfaces we find with the internet of things could have been a first step in that direction. But while computer scientists generally agree that the impact of artificial intelligence needs supervision, they are sceptical when linking the machines' capacity to speak to a more general intelligence or to the rise of consciousness. To them, to anthropomorphize machines and to imagine them as a power-hungry human ego goes a step too far. Discussing the danger of AI, papers such as 'Concrete Problems in AI Safety' (Amodei et al. 2016) connect harmful behaviour to poor design that could lead to accidents and not to an AI gaining its own will. The same thesis can be found with Stuart Russell, Professor of Computer Science at the University of California, Berkeley, who argues that 'the problem isn't consciousness, but competence'. To Russell, the problem looks rather less spectacular than a threatening superintelligence: 'You make machines that are incredibly competent at achieving objectives and they will cause accidents in trying to achieve those objectives' (quoted in Solon 2016a). To those computer scientists, artificial intelligence, including the ability to process natural language, is not the first step of a general intelligence taking over, but rather the entrance into a long, narrow corridor of machines being programmed for very specific tasks. So how can we understand what our things are doing when they speak? Does to have language not also mean to become more human?

To answer that question, let's discuss the problem of our things starting conversations with us from a slightly different perspective. If we start the argument with the fact that the human language *shares* aspects with languages of other species, although it has unique qualities, then machine learning is just *one variety* among many other varieties of language capabilities. Humans were never the only species capable of language. In their article 'The Faculty of Language: What is it, Who Has it, and How Did it Evolve?', Hauser, Chomsky and Fitch (2002) make exactly this point. Their take on human language is 'a comparative approach', linking it to animals, because this 'is most likely to lead to new insights about both shared and derived features' and thus would help to explore 'the design of the faculty of language' further (2002: 1578). Could the faculty of machines to process language be understood in a similar way? If so, communication studies could take up a point recently made in animal studies, which explores the *continuities* between humans and animals, including their shared use of language. Donna Haraway has argued that if non-human animals have language, use tools and exhibit social behaviour, then 'nothing really convincingly settles the separation of human and animal' (Haraway 1991: 152, Haraway 2008). Learning from animal studies then would mean that communication studies would not feel threatened by the fact that technology has started to speak, but would study and understand its very specific language capacity and its power in more detail. Although the processing of natural language might not allow machines to gain a general intelligence, it certainly remains a central skill *for organizing each other socially*, and this is why companies are in peril of risking their reputation with fragile strong ties. So it is important to explore this new machine skill that we experience in our daily lives, instead of leaving this task only to the commercial interests of those companies who currently broaden their influence by making products that speak to us. Exploring this new skill, however, starts with making the effort to understand its general function. For one thing is certain: technology makes progress in processing language. How does the conversational technology that we experience with the internet of things work? And why has it been so difficult until now to get computers to talk to us?

Now we're talking

Humans have been talking to technology for some years now, but for a long time those conversations were often not very pleasant. Stuttering telemarketing robots loading the right statement annoyed us with nuisance calls, despite regulations that should have kept them in check. More helpful (although still annoying) were voice-input and voice-output systems assisting organizations and businesses as digital receptionists to manage and route high call volumes. When dealing with those systems, artificial voices explained to us a menu ('phone tree') by reading lists with topics to choose from. For a long time, limited conversations – single words really – were all that conversational interfaces could process. For what makes language beautiful from a human perspective – that its words and sentences are rich with poetic possibilities and capable of diverse ambiguities – is exactly what poses a problem for a computer. Early in the history of computation, it was understood that processing natural language would be a real test. To this day, different versions of the Turing Test revolve around the question of whether a machine could make conversation in a way indistinguishable from a human. The test was discussed as a research question – whether a computer can master language in such a way that it can imitate a human successfully and thereby 'fool' the human. In the twenty-first century, however, the interests in this test have changed. Today the aim for successful conversations is more pragmatic: a computer that masters human conversation successfully would make life more convenient. It would free our hands and eyes, and would allow users to remotely command a machine – and convenience is one of the most important promises for the adoption of a new technology. Of course, this adoption would also mean that technology companies would enter many more spheres of the human world. When working flawlessly, voice interfaces are known to be intuitive and efficient (Cohen et al. 2004: 10–11; see also Nass & Brave 2005). As computer scientists Hirschberg and Manning point out, 'because natural language represents such a natural interface when interacting' there is 'great commercial interest in the deployment of human language technology' (2015: 261). Whoever cracks the difficulties of natural language processing would gain a market advantage. The task, then, was to teach interfaces to analyse and understand language to generate an enjoyable dialogue. The prize would be an invitation to enter further into our homes and habits. Yet it was not clear if, with the internet of things, technology companies would manage to find a way of processing natural human language, which they had been trying to do for years.

The ambiguity of human language remains one of the most difficult challenges for computer science. Hopes that machines would learn to process natural language had been high ever since the Georgetown experiment in 1954, when a computer managed to translate 60 Russian sentences from punch cards into English following six grammar rules. The range of such a translation, however, was limited. A well-known anecdote from that time is that a literal approach would translate the phrase from the Gospel of Matthew *the spirit indeed is willing, but the flesh is weak* back from Russian into English as *the whisky is agreeable, but the meat has gone bad*. Although such a translation was actually never made by a computer (Hutchins 1995), the sentence demonstrates the fundamental problems computers face when processing language – words are entangled in networks of meanings. Using machine-learning algorithms or decision trees, computer scientists achieved some success, but it was not until the introduction of statistical models that they really made progress in calculating meaning (Charniak 1996). Statistical models have enabled the more pleasant conversations which we now have with our things, by combining new developments in predictive speech recognition and in the parsing of sentences. Both developments made substantial progress when large amounts of language data became available in digital form, so it could be mined; they also used the strategy of 'deep learning' based on neural networks, which calculate numerous examples to infer rules through machine learning (we return to this in chapter 4). Between 2010 and 2015, those methods advanced the field with impressive results (Hirschberg & Manning 2015).

Speech recognition, for example, faced the problem that humans often mumble, or speak with an accent, or find themselves in a loud environment, making it hard for a computer to isolate their syllables. Big Data allowed a solution for this problem: trained on large-sized libraries of natural language, machines learned to predict what is likely to be said based on the surrounding words. In our home assistants and in our smartphones, speech recognition matches the sounds *that can be heard* to the statistical probability of *what could be said*. To be able to calculate what could be said, however, the algorithms work best if they are trained on the parsing of words or sentences as that allows them to analyse the specific role a word has. Understanding the role of words in a sentence is essential to isolate the 'named entities' of a sentence – that is, the people, places or organizations around which meaning usually revolves.

When voice interfaces became gadgets for the mainstream, one of the most advanced parsing algorithms for the English language had just been published by Google. Using a neural network framework called *SyntaxNet*, Google had developed a program called *Parsey McParseface*, which managed to recover individual dependencies between English words with an accuracy of 94 per cent (Petrov 2016). Other spoken dialogue systems such as Siri, Alexa or Cortana were trained on similar frameworks, crunching numerous examples to learn the complex rules of natural language and master them – or at least in part. That language systems became better at processing language does not yet mean they can hold an open conversation. They were, however, becoming good at having a conversation around very specific tasks such as turning the lights on and off, adjusting the room temperature, looking up directions and traffic, playing a specific song or podcast, writing and sending a text message to someone, or politely excusing themselves for not getting it, thereby pointing you to the web. In fact, for a pleasant conversation with our things, the most important task that voice interfaces had to learn was to master misunderstandings. The reason for this is simple: at times, voice interfaces would not be able to deliver a correct answer. Now they could at least offer a polite conversation and make themselves useful by searching the internet for the keyword in your question in order to proudly claim: *Here is what I found for you . . .*

When first entering the mainstream market, their skills could be mapped as follows. In commanding things, Alexa and Siri were the most skilful. As the first real home assistant, Alexa integrated the communication to things right from the start, its other strength being entertainment due to its close connection to the streaming service Amazon Prime. Alexa's weakness, naturally, was the accomplishment of communicative tasks such as sending texts or emails, although it was praised for its jokes. The Google Home assistant aimed to catch up by using its head start in processing language. Google had experimented with speech recognition early on; users could dictate their search queries instead of typing them into their mobile devices or in the Chrome browser's web search (Burke 2008, Singhal 2011). In addition to speech recognition, Google was strong in processing real-time information ever since it managed to embed live-traffic into its Google Maps (Wang 2007). Even more important, however, was that it could learn from search, which had led Google to enrich 'named entities' with contextual facts to create 'knowledge graphs' (Singhal 2012). It is not very surprising that during a test run in 2014, Google Now returned twice as many search results as Siri and nearly three times as many results as Cortana (Enge 2014). Years later, some still regarded Google Now as the best-informed virtual assistant (Chen 2016), and its home assistant would profit from this conversational strength. Microsoft's Cortana struggled longest to reach out to networked things, waiting for one of Microsoft's protocols to be released. It could, however, recognize and identify music and answer questions using Satori, a semantic database of knowledge entities established for Microsoft's search engine Bing. Not having a semantic database of its own, Apple's Siri had to help itself to third-party knowledge by sampling different services, among them WolframAlpha, Wikipedia, Yahoo and Bing (Enge 2014). Adding the framework protocol HomeKit to Siri in 2014, however, allowed the assistant to gather experience in controlling thermostats and air quality, lights, shades or door locks before any of its competitors could do this. Moreover, Apple had understood more quickly than its competitors that a conversational tone could make up for problems – among all artificial intelligence assistants Siri draws most on having a persona. Here again we find the combination of algorithms, agency and anthropomorphism: having a conversation with a technical device is new territory. While the technical processing of words is one problem, designing a personality that we actually want to speak to is another one. And to a certain extent, the question of personality is key when making attempts to organize how we interact with things.

Human listeners automatically infer from voices a fictional personality. Experts have stated that 'the entire field of research that sociolinguists call *speech evaluation* strongly suggests that there is no such thing as a voice user interface without personality' (Cohen et al. 2004: 75). We categorize the emotional status of a voice (excited, sad, happy) and merge it with potential social cues such as accent, age or gender. Thus, voice interface designers are tasked with creating a human-like persona in correspondence with the assistant's task. Users struggle with inconsistencies. They expect the type of voice, its tone and its vocabulary to match (Nass & Brave 2005: 50), as well as to find a relation between persona and its task. In short, they are looking for human behaviour. While the voice interface of a bank should speak in a polite and impersonal tone, the artificial intelligence assistants in our homes or on our phones generally speak to us in a more familiar manner, and their dialogue design has prompt scripts that make them tell jokes or react to emotional statements. Confronted with the slightly confused statement 'I don't know', Siri replies 'Don't worry about it, Mercedes'; when asked 'Talk dirty to me', it answers 'The carpet needs vacuum cleaning'. By engineering human elements – humour, manners and emotions – into the conversation, Siri has been the showcase for a human-like persona using playfulness to establish not only a dialogue, but a conversation. And the more 'natural' the dialogue, experts hope, the more an interface can make use of the fact that we are 'wired for speech', as Clifford Nass and Scott Brave have put it. In their book exploring how the evolving human–computer relationship is using voice, they argue:

> When voice interfaces fully leverage how humans are wired for speech, users will not simply talk at and listen to computers, nor will computers simply talk *at* and listen *to* users. Instead, people and computers will cooperatively *speak with* one another. (Nass & Brave 2005: 184)

The internet of things has proved them right. As we humans *are* 'wired for speech', more and more fluent conversations have imbued things further with agency. However, our recent history suggests that fluency in conversation might not even be necessary. Instead, we seem to be willing to accept a thing's pre-scripted opinion already when it just talks *at* us – at least in specific situations such as driving a car.

Do what you're told?

When their satnav told three Japanese tourists travelling in Australia that there was a road from the mainland to North Stradbroke Island, 15 km away, they drove into the Pacific Ocean. They simply kept driving, even though there was no road, until they got stuck in the mud, their car flooded by the tide. After being rescued, driver Yuzu Noda told a local newspaper that their car's navigation system was to blame: 'It told us we could drive down there', she told reporters. 'It kept saying it would navigate us to a road' (Freak & Holloway 2012). While driving into the ocean is an extreme case, these drivers are not alone in obeying the commands of their car's conversational technology in the face of obvious evidence to the contrary. In the UK, a driver continued to follow the satnav's instructions when it told him the narrow, steep path he was driving on in Todmorden, West Yorkshire was a road. He was willing to notice the mistake only after he found his BMW was hanging off the edge of a cliff. In South Brunswick, New Jersey, a driver ignored the end of a road displayed differently on his navigation system. Following the satnav's version of reality, he ignored a stop sign and hit a house. In Bergun, Switzerland, the navigation system told a man to turn onto a trail. The trail was for goats.

The minivan, which he had driven up that trail, could only reach the road again with the help of a heavy-lift helicopter. In Belgium, a woman tried to use her satnav to get to the train station in her home-town, and kept following its instructions for 900 miles until she reached Zagreb in Croatia.

Cars were among the first of our things to operate in a connected mode. Long before a navigation system had become an inherent part of a car, they gave verbal advice to drivers on how to reach a destina-tion. When it comes to the effects of voice interfaces, cars provide us with early experiences to learn from – not all of them good. Ever since the introduction of navigation systems into the car market in the 1980s, the adventures of humans who trusted their car's navigation systems have become a genre in their own right – and a global phenomenon. All over the world, humans have believed their direction-giving assistants more than their own eyes. But note that in all of the above cases the advice of technology could easily have been ignored. Their capacity to speak was far from the skilled conversa-tions digital assistants such as Siri can hold. The system surely could not persuade a human by using skilful rhetoric or impress drivers with their persona. Not following the advice also came with no conse-quences – with Granovetter (1973) one could say that the ties between an external navigation system and a car are rather weak. So how can we explain why the drivers still followed their navigation system? One thing is that in most cases the drivers, often tourists, were not famil-iar with their environment. Thus, they listened to 'their' technology rather than asking other humans for help or accepting the bad news of being lost and having to go back. The drivers decided to follow the advice of the navigation system *despite* what they could see in front of their eyes.

Here, it becomes visible that we humans play our part when it comes to the agency of technology. As difficulties for a minivan on a steep goat trail were predictable, the decision to drive up the mountain was a joint one. If that is the case, the example shows that the agency of technology can be understood as a joint leadership: technology provided advice, and – although other information was available – the human executed it. In such cases technology can be understood as a 'technical ensemble', as the French philosopher Gilbert Simondon put it. Simondon (2017: 17) argued that technology is fundamentally linked to a human: 'The machine endowed with a high degree of technicity is an open machine, and all open machines taken together [l'ensemble des machines ouvertes] presuppose man as their permanent organizer, as the living interpreter.' This point – that a human being is a permanent organizer and living interpreter when it comes to technology – is important; all the more so as it is relevant not just for engineers and tech designers, but also for each of us everyday users. This can be seen in our next example – supermarket self-service checkouts.

Self-service checkouts equipped with a scanner and a pair of scales have become very common in many countries. In the UK, its biggest supermarket chain Tesco started operating them in 2003; twelve years later, 12,000 self-service checkouts could be found in its stores (Tesco 2015). These too are part of the internet of things – they process their received information by being connected to a network, they are equipped with sensors, and they are operated by having a dialogue with their user, the customer, about what to do next. To check if a customer handles all items correctly, most early versions weigh each item after it is taken out of the shopping basket and placed in the grocery bag that generally has to be put on a large scale also known as 'the bagging area'. If anything does not comply with the expected procedure, the checkout starts frantically to advise you. 'Please scan your item', or 'unexpected item in the bagging area – remove this item before continuing'. If the customer fails to do so, the checkout locks down and flashes a light to alarm an assistant. It does this often – the system is rather delicate. Whenever an item is too light or the scale fails to recognize it, the checkout system troubleshoots: it implicitly makes the assumption that you might be a thief, until an assistant unlocks the checkout so you can continue your shopping process. To avoid this, some customers have taken drastic measures – they have started to steal. A UK survey found that almost 20 per cent of customers admitted to stealing from self-service checkouts, with more than half of those saying that they had first started taking goods because they could not get an item to scan (Carter 2014). The findings were echoed by a report from the University of Leicester, which found that some shoppers deliberately bag some items without scanning them, leading to loss rates for the shop that were 122 per cent higher than in contexts where staff scanned items at the checkout (Beck & Hopkins 2015). A later study coined the term SWIPERS, an acronym for 'Seemingly Well-Intentioned Patrons Engaging in Routine Shoplifting', and identified irritation and frustration with the scanning interface as one cause of shoplifting (Taylor 2016). Being verbally harassed by the nagging of the checkout device, the communication between technical thing and human had an unforeseen effect. The checkout device had initiated a very different relationship between user and shop than Tesco had intended. Tesco finally decided to change its checkout's communication strategy in 2015, perhaps for those reasons. In a press release it acknowledged that 'the current voice has become a source of frustration for customers, with some describing it as "shouty" and "irritating", and putting them under pressure as they finish their shop' (Tesco 2015). Instead of warning that an unexpected item could be found in the bagging area, it then went for the less technical advice: *this can now be placed in your bag*. Users soon recognized, however, that the much bigger change was not the wording but the gender exchange of the checkout persona – the 'irritating' female voice had been replaced with a male one. To reorganize the relationship of the user to the machine, the company suggested a different way of anthropomorphizing the cashier, thereby wittingly or unwittingly reinforcing gender prejudices.

When voice interface designers shape conversations, they incorporate expectations about accent, age and gender. For example, it is therefore not very surprising that IBM's question-answering computer system *Watson* had been equipped with a *male* voice fitting its task to win the quiz show *Jeopardy!* which it finally achieved in 2011. Testing showed that a male voice was considered more adequate for the mansplaining the computer had to do when playing the quiz, even though the IBM team had originally supported a female version (Markoff 2016). In a paper looking into the conversation style of Amazon's home assistant Alexa, Charles Hannon (2016) pointed out that the female voice of Alexa, on the other hand, had been programmed to signal a lower status in the relationship with the speaker: Alexa was designed to take the blame for any miscommunication.

When not understanding a question, for example, Alexa's response was to say *I didn't understand the question that I heard* instead of indicating *I didn't understand your question*. While the last sentence leaves open whether the reason for the misunderstanding is with the questioner or the hearer, Alexa offers that the device might have heard it the wrong way. By linking Alexa's answers to the linguistic studies of James Pennebaker on language patterns, Charles Hannon could show that the response of the digital assistant reinforces a gender-bias – it is not a coincidence that the default voice for many home assistants is female. Analysing over 14,000 language samples, Pennebaker found that 14.2 per cent of women's words were personal pronouns compared with only 12.7 per cent of men's; and regardless of the gender of the people communicating, the person perceived to have lower status uses the first pronoun *I* more often. In both cases, the style of speaking makes it clear that the person is indicating a very personal approach to the world instead of a general one. Observations like these led Hannon to call for a more conscious design of AI that is aware of identity politics: 'efforts to create a more equal language pattern in our AIs' as they 'subvert or circumvent those [patterns] we find more generally in the world' (Hannon 2016: 35). One might think that 'machine learning' could be a way out of this human mess as it is a technology in which machines teach themselves the usage of language by processing large amounts of data. Unfortunately, tests have shown the opposite. Machine-learning systems trained on Google News articles have exhibited gender stereotypes to a disturbing extent, further amplifying biases and making it necessary for computer scientists to adjust them (Bolukbasi et al. 2016). Indeed, systems that can be taught to detect abusive language are currently being explored (Waseem et al. 2017) – and bots such as Microsoft's Tay could soon be able to acquire manners.

Conclusion

Having been equipped with a voice, the things around us have started to speak to us. This has changed our understanding of communication. We are no longer just using media to send and receive messages with other humans, but have also started to have meaningful conversations with digital technology. Driven by new technological advancements such as deep learning, our connected things can match the sounds that can be heard to the statistical probability of what would be said. While this skill makes our things appear smart, it is also a way to organize certain interests. Wired for speech, we anthropomorphize technology. By providing it with a persona, however, we automatically assume a certain role within that dialogue. To critically monitor and explore those roles and their negative but also potentially positive effects is a task of communication studies curious to explore the speaking of things. A few days after users managed to turn Microsoft's chatbot Tay into a racist, Nazi-sympathizing troll, the company released its framework to enable users to build their own bots (Microsoft Bot Framework 2016). There will be no lack of conversations.

4

Seeing things

The first fatal crash of a self-driving car involved a failure of algorithmic sight. The crash left its driver, Joshua Brown, dead. On the day, the autopilot system of his Tesla Model S car navigated the highway by means of cameras, radar, ultrasonic sensors and computer software. It did so automatically – cars too are now part of the internet of things. They have become networked, addressed objects that are packed with sensors. The navigational functions of the Model S vehicle relied on especially sophisticated sensors: surround cameras with 360° vision and image recognition software; ultrasonic scanners to detect objects ahead; radar and GPS with real-time traffic information; and all processed by an onboard networked computer able to download software and firmware updates over the air, and controlled by a touch-screen (Tesla 2016a). But in this case, the system did not distinguish the white side of a tractor trailer from the clear sky behind it. Brown's self-driving car crashed into the much larger vehicle at a crossing, as the trailer made a left turn across its path. The car drove full speed under the trailer, its top torn off by the force of the collision, before continuing its ride off the road, hitting a fence and a power pole and coming to a stop. Despite Tesla's instructions that drivers need to keep their eyes on the road and their hands on the wheel, Brown had trusted the vehicle's networked system, relying on his car to do the actual driving for him – so much so that some news reports suggested he might have been watching a Harry Potter movie on a portable DVD player when his car crashed (Levin & Woolf 2016). The self-driving car's manufacturer, Tesla Motors, called the incident 'a tragic loss', stating that their autopilot system had been activated by drivers for a total of more than 130 million miles, and this was the first known fatal accident. Tesla suggested that this was still better than the average for normal cars, which it said was a fatality every 94 million miles in the US, or every 60 million miles worldwide (Tesla 2016b). But Joshua Brown was dead. The incident showed that the dream of self-driving cars, watching and aware of the world around them, was more complicated than some had thought. It highlighted the difficulties of giving the sense of sight to things.

Connected things have learned to see with their own eyes. Equipped with lasers, radar, sensors and cameras, they make sense of the world around them. They know how to find their way and can spot you standing behind them. They identify dangerous situations, inform you about the coffee being ready or warn you that someone is breaking into your house. But they may also mistake a baby playing with a toothbrush for a young boy holding a baseball bat. They have shown racist tendencies by being unable to recognize black people. And they may kill a driver by failing to distinguish a white truck against a bright summer sky.

This chapter looks at the *computer vision* of networked things. It first discusses how the internet of things has long been bound up with technologies of visibility, looking at some of the first connected things – webcams. It then examines one of the most developed cases of the internet of things – cars – as an example of how things see and make sense of the world, discussing challenges and progress made in computer vision. Finally, it shows that computer vision has *inbuilt politics*: while computer vision enables networked things to become more autonomous, it also equips them with the ability to see or to serve particular groups, experiences, ideas or topics. In other words, their ability to see might – consciously or unconsciously – be ideologically fixated, making *media recognition* a communication subject to study next to *media representation*.

Technologies of visibility

Before media could recognize, they simply made things visible. The original idea of the webcam used visibility as a form of communication – it allowed scientists to monitor a coffee machine. In late 1991, computing researchers at the University of Cambridge pointed an old video camera at their coffee machine and displayed its feed using a script that allowed each of them to see from their computer screen whether there was any fresh coffee left. The idea, as so often with the internet of things, was to solve a problem of convenience: those whose offices were several flights of stairs away from the coffee often missed out to those who worked close enough to smell a fresh pot from its location in the Trojan Room. The image was transmitted through the building's local network using a special program written to do so. With the launch of the first graphical browser, *Mosaic*, in 1993, monitoring the Trojan Room coffee pot became accessible to any web user. The web had its first webcam. The novelty and the very banality of the image brought millions of viewers to the coffee pot feed over the years (Stafford-Fraser n.d., Kirksey 2005: 100).

Here, the networked webcam is both a technology of visibility and an early component of the internet of things. In one sense, all media are technologies of visibility, in that they make something visible that was previously invisible – from the shared stories of a national culture given collage form in the daily newspaper (Anderson 1991) to the simultaneous, shared attention of broadcasting (Dayan 2009), developments in communication technology have brought new experiences of social visibility. As the telegraph brought information at the speed of electricity (Carey 1989), and as photography enabled the recording of new forms of durable personal history (Barthes 1981), so too does the webcam make visible what could before not be seen with ease, and it does this in ways that precede our understanding of sensing networks. The webcam is therefore an early example of a networked peripheral device, and of one that extends the user's sensory range. It offers a familiar example for comparison with some of the more experimental developments which this chapter discusses as the skill of *seeing things*. With the webcam, ordinary users began to connect *things* – cameras – to the internet and they used those things to create and distribute information. Moreover, the webcam is a technology of visibility, and visibility – sensing and seeing – is a central element of the internet of things.

To apply vision to a thing to make it act autonomously is an old robotic dream. If things could gain the skill of seeing the world around them, they would gain orientation and act more autonomously. But providing things with eyes by applying a camera or a radar only solves half of the problem. After getting the images, they also need to be able to analyse and interpret them correctly – a problem that computer scientists have been eager to solve. In teaching things to understand images, cars have been one of the favourite test beds for this so-called 'computer vision'. The reason for this is that the actions required of a car are limited. Cars drive on streets from A to B. While driving, what they need to look out for is more or less clear and this turns the vision needed for automated driving into a programmable task. Vision can only be programmed if the conditions and actions of a connected thing are definable. This means that computer vision never sees the whole picture, but only what it is *programmed to look out for*. Computer engineers try to understand precisely what a connected thing needs in order to pursue its activities, and then program its sight accordingly. When driving, cars have to react to the route of the road, mind the traffic rules, and avoid any collision with obstacles.

Computer engineers at both car companies and technology companies anticipate benefits from this. Besides a reduction in traffic, the most important one is the reduction in traffic collisions resulting in fewer deaths and injuries, and also a reduction in costs. To those engineers, developing an autopilot system that can avoid collisions is simply the next logical step in a safety development race that started with the rapidly inflating airbag cushion to reduce crash impact. Next came power-assisted steering or anti-lock braking systems to help the driver in manoeuvring the car more effectively. Then parts of the driving process were automated, starting with parking, and once sensors could visually and audibly display distances, they could also allow the car to park all by itself. Now those sensors could also be used for a very different function: they could detect an imminent collision and warn the driver, or even brake without the driver's input – computers can react much faster than humans, at least if they spot the threat correctly. This list shows that to car engineers, the aim of reducing fatalities and costs is nothing new. Step by step – in a race for safety, to assist the driver, or to take over routine tasks – the car was being developed into a sensing thing. Finally, it came to the core task that we do when we get into a car: driving.

Approaches differed in how to create a fully connected self-driving car. Many companies pushed into this new territory with different strategies, from car companies such as Ford, Toyota or BMW to transportation services such as Uber. The two companies which established the car as a networked thing first, Google and Tesla, followed very different approaches. Tesla, an American automotive and energy storage company, had decided to develop self-driving features for their electric cars. For this, they frequently released more and more autonomous and semi-autonomous software assisting with specific tasks that was still in beta testing. To drivers, it was a cool although obviously dangerous feature, the more so as changing into autopilot mode did not come each time with a warning, but was as easy as switching on a car's lights. To Tesla, it meant that they could test their self-driving features in real conditions and with real drivers. Here Tesla, despite being a car company, applied a strategy practised in software development – *release early, release often* – which emphasizes a tight feedback loop between developers and users. Bit by bit, different aspects of driving a Tesla Model S car were assisted or replaced over time: an automatic emergency braking system, automatic parallel parking, automatic emergency steering and side collision warning, auto lane change and automatic steering to keep the car in the same lane. Combined, the many different functions would allow a car to drive itself in many situations. Instead of doing the actual driving, the engagement of the human behind the steering wheel was now required to monitor and test the self-driving features so that Tesla could gather extensive data. Sucking in its users' data, the car had become part of the internet of things.

Google, on the other hand, went for a different strategy. It tested its self-driving car extensively. For this, specially trained drivers commanded a small fleet of modified Lexus SUVs with the goal of making themselves replaceable. By the time of Joshua Brown's fatal crash, Google's test vehicles had logged only 1.5 million miles, compared to Tesla's 130 million. Unlike Tesla, Google was not interested in developing self-driving features to assist drivers of recognizable cars. Instead, they were working towards a quite new kind of vehicle that could drive itself from place to place without any human intervention. Although Google announced at that time that it was not interested in producing cars, the company did present a model to visualize its dream. Its self-driving prototype, unveiled in May 2014, was a two-seater with no steering wheel, no accelerator, no brake pedal or mirrors. Their car was not to be driven by faulty humans but by functioning computers. Perhaps to allay any concerns, it was given a rather infantile design – its front lights and sensors made it look like a sad koala. Or was it to reflect the fact that much like other companies, Google struggled to apply a truly fail-safe vision? In any case, it seemed companies had run into difficulties when developing a vision for things. So when and how would things really learn to see? To illustrate the skill of seeing that the things around us were programmed to acquire, the next section of this chapter provides a short overview of the most important breakthroughs in image recognition and computer vision at that time, thereby explaining its techniques, and where this technique failed.

Seeing is believing

The sense of sight is difficult to program. The reason for this is because seeing is twofold: for a human, the sense of sight is not something that concerns just our eyes. Having vision means to be able *to visually perceive the world*: from a functional perspective, to make sense is to be able to arrive at an appropriate motor or cognitive response. The purpose of the visual process is a vision that mediates cognition and motion. This is why the human visual system, developed largely after birth in the first few years of life, involves both the brain and the eye. The brain is an essential part of identifying what it is that we see and of making sense of it. Even if we cannot see an object fully or clearly, we often know what it is that we find in front of our eyes. The brain fills in the missing information. In other words, we are not just seeing with our eyes. When imitating this ability, computer vision faces a problem. Technical sensors might detect more, reach deeper and offer a wider range than the human eye, but they need to be programmed to make sense of what it is that they see so clearly: their visual sight needs to be assisted by image recognition. They need to correctly identify what is in the image that the sensors have recorded. Only when recognizing shapes in images and being able to identify those shapes, do things start 'to see'. This correct identification, however, was part of a massive challenge computer scientists were facing.

Figure 4.1. All images are as ambiguous to untrained computer systems as the duck-rabbit.

Computers do not see the world as we do. Unless a software program advises them to look for specific forms and shades that could mean something, they find themselves in front of a lot of pixels that could mean anything. Perhaps it helps to explain the problem computers have with an example from human sight: optical illusions. Optical illusions occur when we see a picture which we struggle to identify clearly, such as the sketch shown in figure 4.1. The 'duck-rabbit', may be known to some as the example Ludwig Wittgenstein (2009: 204) uses to discuss the specificity of human perception. It can be seen as either a rabbit's head or a duck's head, although not at the same time.

Seeing in the mode of an optical illusion describes untrained computer vision: computers simply face patterns that could be a lot of different things. To identify an actual entity in those patterns – a face, a car, a cyclist, a cat or a roast chicken – computer software looks for typical pixel formations. They look for the pixel formations of fur to narrow a possible entity down to the category of animals, or they look for the formation of a leaf to narrow a possible entity down to outdoor flora, and so on. By finding edges, or specific regions of colour, programs manage to identify skin, shapes and components. Looking at colour and colour shades, edges and angles, they calculate possible identifications and come up with the most likely one: that what can be seen in an image is probably a furred animal or a tree or a face. When recognizing a face, for example, computer vision looks for its typical attributes: two eyes, a nose and a mouth arranged in a typical manner, as well as coming with a specific range of colours. Human faces are rarely green or blue, unless perhaps they are going to a football game wearing face paint – and this exception demonstrates some of the problems for computer vision. And there are more: when people eat something or speak into a phone, they perform actions that visually interfere with the typical shape of a face, thereby confusing computer vision.

For a long time, teaching vision to a computer meant programming the right rules to detect shapes and shades that define an object. Those rule-based systems knew that a stop sign is octagonal and red and has the word STOP written on it. Or a cat has a round head with pointed ears and a tail. In real life, however, each object comes in an infinite number of variations. Take the cat. As documented in great detail on the internet, cats are extremely bendable. Could a computer camera spot the animal halfway hidden behind a couch? Or in the middle of an action such as jumping or yawning? Or lying on a tiger-striped sofa cover? The camera might also film the cat from an unusual perspective or in an insufficient light that displays a cat's reflective eyes. In the early days of programming recognition systems, researchers tried to come up with rules for what an object could be and to add all possible exceptions. But they struggled. For use in an actual internet of things device, let alone for driving a car, the failure rate for correctly identifying objects in an image was too high. A different approach was necessary.

The solution was the following: instead of programming the rules that a computer should apply when analysing images, its recognition system would be programmed to look at correctly labelled images in order *to infer the rules of identification*. In other words, the computer was not programmed to follow specific rules of identification, but learned from observational data – it was shown correct material from which it would then create rules. For computer vision, this approach would become known as *neural network image classification* (Kung & Taur 1995), which is based on the machine-learning paradigm of 'neural networks'. A neural network is an architecture that allows computer programs to infer rules and is therefore open to complexity. This biologically inspired paradigm consists of several layers, each made up of many individual artificial neurons, which individually analyse different aspects of evidence before passing on to the next neuron or layer. By making each node and layer combine their calculation power, the program can look at numerous tiny aspects, inviting complexity – a complexity that can be confusing, even for a computer. The systems are not easy to program as they can get lost in that complexity. For example, they can focus too much on learning the specifics of the training data instead of generalizing from them. When looking at new and unseen data, the model then fails as it is 'overfitting'. If these systems work, however, they provide astonishing results. But to train neural networks in this mode of 'deep learning', computer scientists needed a large data bank of images – a problem that would be solved with the help of ordinary internet users.

When we users started uploading images at the beginning of the twenty-first century, we made billions of pictures available. Our urge to share our lives online produced excellent training material for computer scientists. They then produced image-language datasets on which the objects displayed in our images were correctly named. In the UK, a dataset known as 'PASCAL Voc' was created that allowed computers to train on 11,530 annotated images. This was surpassed by the Flickr30k set with over 30,000 pictures focusing on people and everyday activities, and Microsoft's MS COCO consisting of 300,000 images offering multiple objects per image, which challenges computers to identify more than just one thing; and finally by an even larger dataset, ImageNet (Deng et al. 2009), which provided over 1 million images with annotations. Creating datasets to teach things to see, however, was a challenge of its own. Computer scientists needed to further process our pictures, once downloaded. They had to ensure that the pictures were correctly labelled, for example. For this tedious task known as 'cleaning the data', ImageNet and other computer vision research projects turned to Amazon's micro-task marketplace Mechanical Turk (Karpathy & Fei-Fei 2015). In fact, ImageNet was at its peak one of Mechanical Turk's biggest employers. According to Fei-Fei Li, at that time director of the Stanford Artificial Intelligence Lab, which was hosting the project, 48,940 people in 167 countries sorted and labelled nearly a billion images downloaded from the internet. They had helped to create the material (see figure 4.2) necessary to train computers to see. And indeed, computer scientists could report progress.

In 2010, ImageNet hosted for the first time the annual 'ImageNet

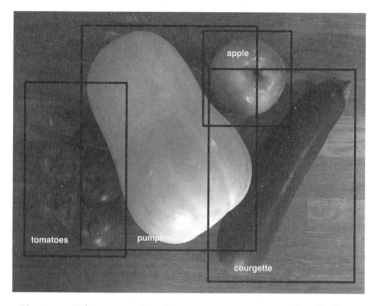

Figure 4.2. When annotating pictures, computer systems identify objects on an image.

Large Scale Visual Recognition Challenge', in which state-of-the-art technology competed to correctly classify and detect objects and scenes. The outcomes were promising, but at over 25 per cent the error rates were still high. Early test examples showed they could correctly identify pictures such as *a man in black shirt is playing guitar* or *a baseball player is throwing the ball in a game*, but the trained software was failing to understand others (Karpathy & Fei-Fei 2015). A picture showing a baby lying on its back playing with a toothbrush was identified as *a young boy is holding a baseball bat*; another picture showing a woman and a man pouting at the camera from behind a white Apple laptop even became *a woman holding a teddy bear in front of a mirror* (Karpathy n.d.). Although quite amusing, a system with such an error rate would face difficulties when operating in the real world, not to mention being allowed to drive.

But in 2012 a different approach emerged. The research team of the University of Toronto tweaked the framework of their object recognition system (Krizhevsky et al. 2012). Their different approach increased the performance, effectively crushing their competition by being 10 per cent more accurate – a success that took neural networks 'from obscure models that were shrouded in skepticism to rockstars of Computer Vision' (Karpathy 2015). This success came through fine-tuning the framework of neural networks further. Like other neural networks, their neuron-nodes looked at the same image independently of each other, each searching for different aspects: edges, skin tones or lines, for example, that were then merged with higher nodes to predict what could be seen. But to assist the learning process, the computer scientists had encoded specific image properties into the network architecture directly, thereby making its nodes work together in a more effective way. Impressed by the first success, more and more research labs explored this approach and year after year the error rate when classifying pictures became smaller and smaller. In 2014, Google's system GoogLeNet could present an error rate of just 6.7 per cent on a full test set of 100,000 images (Szegedy 2014). In the following year, Microsoft's team managed to reduce this further, achieving an error rate of 4.94 per cent; the error rate of a trained human in comparison was estimated to be 5.1 per cent (Karpathy 2014). Could computer programs now equip our things with the ability to see?

If computers had learned the skill of seeing, they surely saw the world with different eyes, as a test run by Google engineers showed. To check if their neural network had correctly learned to look out for the right features (Mordvintsev et al. 2015), a group of engineers decided to turn the learning procedure upside down: instead of letting a computer learn by showing images with objects, they told the recognition system to depict an object including its most important features. For this, the system started with random pixels, which it tweaked in colours and shapes until it had created what it thought was the object it had been told to visualize (see figure 4.3).

In most cases the neural network was able to come up with the correct shape and shade of an object. At times, however, it seemed to have misunderstood. When asked to produce the image of a dumbbell, the neural network suggested a weightlifting arm attached to it. The plausible explanation the engineers suggested was that

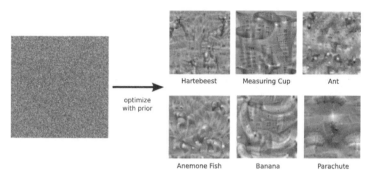

Figure 4.3. Google's neural network depicting shapes from random noise.

'maybe it's never been shown a dumbbell without an arm holding it' (Mordvintsev et al. 2015).

Still, the test could prove that recognition systems had indeed learned to process still images. Inspired by the progress computer vision had made, computer engineers also started to develop ideas to apply those skills. It was not just the self-driving car – other things also learnt to see, although in the beginning their application of vision was sometimes a little bit obscure. For example, software engineer Kurt Grandis used algorithmic sight to solve his squirrel problem – the agile animals had taken over the bird house in his backyard. By applying an Open Source Computer Vision to a water gun, the system was trained to 'see'. It could detect squirrels and differentiate them from birds, and would then target and shoot at the bushy-tailed food thieves, an approach Grandis (2012) introduced with a wink as 'Militarizing your Backyard with Python: Computer Vision and the Squirrel Hordes'. A more serious approach was Photonic Fence (n.d.) to fight malaria. Here, the skill of seeing was to be used to identify insects as they crossed a virtual fence. Reading the input of the sensors that formed this fence, algorithms could estimate the insect's size and measure its wingbeat frequency to determine if it was a friendly bumblebee or a hostile mosquito. After a safety check, it would then activate a laser to zap the mosquito. The skill of seeing would also become important for medical devices, a research area for which computer vision has been especially promising: new heart rate monitors started to simply 'see' the pulse of a person. Simply by looking at a video feed of a person, computer programs would magnify subtle changes of colour that revealed the blood flow (Olsen 2013). Other programs were examining 2D or 3D medical data such as lung CT images, in which they looked for tiny early-stage nodules (El-Baz et al. 2013). And forgetful people could identify pills with the help of a pill identification app on their smartphone. Of course, this could only be used after they agreed to the terms of service that ensured the app provider would take no responsibility for wrongly identified pills. But among the more and more devices that applied the skills of seeing, the most promising approach was still to make cars able to move more autonomously.

When cars learned to see, one thing was obvious to engineers right from the start. Instead of developing one single technology, they would need to merge different information feeds from different sensors, both new and pre-recorded. Google tested self-driving car systems in an urban environment early on, and combined all the information to analyse the situation the car found itself in: there was a powerful Velodyne LiDAR radar mounted on top of the car, which performed laser distance measurement to generate a detailed 3D map of its environment at a range of 60–100 m (Solon 2016b); it also performed object detection. Further, bumper-mounted radar kept track of vehicles directly in front of and behind the car (GreyB 2014). And it came equipped with a standard camera that pointed through the windscreen. Software combining the information feeds of cameras and sensors could then identify pedestrians, cyclists and other motorists who might become hazards; it could also read road signs and detect traffic lights, and had learned to distinguish vehicles to identify the shape of school buses (slow down) or the flashing light of police cars (make room so it can pass by; pull over on request). The program matched what it saw live to high-precision digital recordings of the same street created beforehand. One can imagine those recordings much like those of Google's Street View project, only with a better resolution and further annotated to mark road lanes, traffic lights, traffic signs and other aspects important to a driving car (Waymo 2016). Only new objects needed to be identified, which were then linked to pre-learned behaviour patterns: for example with the rule that a cyclist who extends the left arm needs some space to turn safely, so the car should slow down.

Such a pattern could go wrong: the first accident that Google's self-driving car caused occurred on 14 February 2016 and was linked to applying the wrong behaviour to a public transit bus. The self-driving car assumed that the bus approaching from behind had not enough space to pass it while waiting in a lane to turn. Thinking it was obstructing the lane, and applying the behaviour pattern *will slow down* to the bus, it pulled out, driving into the centre of the lane to pass some sandbags on the street that were blocking its path. But the public transit bus driver knew his vehicle well. When approaching from behind, he was sure that there would be sufficient space. The bus was just about to pass the self-driving car, when it pulled out and hit the bus in the side at 2 miles an hour; the bus was travelling at 15 miles an hour. Incidents like these show that the difficulties in making the car 'understand', as Google put it, were more complex than assumed – and companies developing self-driving cars soon came to acknowledge that. Whenever the shapes and shades around those cars were not clearly distinct, they failed. They had problems when spotting the course of a road in snow and in other weather conditions. Or they failed to identify a white lorry against a brightly lit spring sky. Whenever visual differences were minimal, the software programs of cars had a problem. We would therefore see self-driving cars first for regions blessed with sunny weather and wide-open roads, was the conclusion of Chris Urmson, the director of Google's self-driving car project at that time, who said in a public talk: 'cars might be sold for those markets first' (2016b). But despite the challenges and setbacks, the belief that computer vision could be programmed to see better than the human, and should drive instead of the human, was strong. A certain sense of the superiority of technology could indeed be found in the public statements of those companies.

The agency of things

For years, the argument for automation has been that a machine can do a task better than a human. A machine is quicker, faster, cheaper, and can act more efficiently. This is an argument which is also often made about the internet of things: being connected to lots of data, things know more, they see or sense their environment better, and they can react faster than a human. In other words, by being connected things gain a new and more efficient kind of *agency*. When it comes to self-driving cars, for example, companies such as Google and Tesla are promising that the non-human agency of their cars will diminish accidents. And this seems to make sense. Self-driving cars do not get distracted by messages on their phones or screaming requests for attention from their kids, and would surely never drive drunk. Self-driving cars are more reliable than a human actor would be because they are non-human actors. But is this really the case? To explore this question further, we turn to the approach of Critical Discourse Analysis (Fairclough 2003, Machin & Mayr 2012, Hansen & Machin 2013, Wodak 2013) and to the public arguments companies such as Tesla and Google make when discussing their cars. Understanding language as a form of social practice, we analyse their arguments and look at the discursive positioning of human and non-human agents and their relation. Tesla Motors, for example, when responding to Joshua Brown's fatal accident, defended its project as follows:

> This is the first known fatality in just over 130 million miles where Autopilot was activated. Among all vehicles in the US, there is a fatality every 94 million miles. Worldwide, there is a fatality approximately every 60 million miles. (Tesla 2016b)

By claiming *that there is a fatality every 94 million miles*, after having stated that *this is the first known fatality in just over 130 million miles*, the implied argument is made: *so the development of autopilot systems should continue*. Although they were shocked about the *tragic loss* in which their autopilot system was involved, they insisted in the same post that autonomous driving cars would be less flawed than human drivers. A similar argument can be found in the description of Google's self-driving car project by its then-project leader Chris Urmson:

> Deadly car crashes surged in the first half of 2015 [. . .] with experts projecting that deaths may have topped 40,000 for the year. It's the equivalent of a 737 full of passengers falling out of the sky five days a week, all year long, yet we seem to accept this as the price of our mobility. Self-driving cars have the potential to reduce those numbers, because they eliminate the driver inattention and

error that leads to thousands of collisions, injuries, and deaths – in fact, 94% of crashes are caused by human error. (Urmson 2016a)

Again, the boundaries of human and non-human are very clear: *94% of crashes are caused by human error*, and it is *technology*, a *non-human* agent, that has the potential to reduce this number.

When pointing out the human error, Google's and Tesla's descriptions of the situation follow a subtle dialectic. Both describe the automated system as a different category – *non-human* – and as such less fallible. The agency of cars is here what is desired for the future. At first sight, it does not seem very surprising that cars can have agency, especially not from the perspective of cultural studies. Here, theories in which things play a distinct role have as a fact become more numerous. That things have agency and should be seen as actors resonates well with a turn our discourse took at the end of the twentieth century. The following short list illustrates this rise and the importance of this topic in our contemporary discourse, although it is by no means exhaustive. Its function here is rather to deliver a rough overview to those interested in studying theories of thing agency further. Among others, it has been suggested that *things* can be read:

- As imbued with social agency. Looking at art objects and beyond, the anthropologist Alfred Gell (1998: 18–19) described things as forms of instrumental action to point out that social agency is not only exercised by people but 'can be exercised by "things" ', which 'can appear as "agents" in particular social situations'. For Gell, the agency of things is the result of an invested human agency.
- As an *actant*. The sociologist Bruno Latour takes Gell's approach one step further. Criticizing the traditional subject–object dichotomy that splits the human world into an active subject and a passive object, Latour (1992) uses the example of his car nagging him to fasten his seatbelt, besides other examples (1991, 1993, 2000). For Latour 'technology is society made durable' (1991), which means our world is made up of human and non-human 'actants' (a word intended to elide the difference between the two). This post-humanist approach, which became known as Actor-Network Theory (2005), focuses less on the autonomy of things, instead reading them as part of an association made up of humans and

non-humans. Recently, Noortje Marres specified the agency of actants further by showing that things have a political potential she describes as an 'issuefication' (Marres 2014).

- As autonomous. While Bill Brown (2001, 2004) also explores the human–object interactions, he often approaches things and their autonomy from the perspective of art and culture. Following Heidegger's distinction between objects and things (2001), he looks at the thingness exposed when the functioning of an object breaks down.
- As entangled. Both Tim Ingold (2010) and Ian Hodder (2012) turn their attention towards the connection things have and their entanglements with contexts, processes and meanings. Hodder's extensive study (2012) shows a strong emphasis on the matter of things and their temporality and argues that the interrelationship of humans and things is a defining characteristic of human history. To Ingold, things, other than objects, are also not passive or still-objects but need to be understood as processes gathering together threads of life.
- As non-humans. Recent efforts to arrive at a post-human perspective have partly been based on writing theory from the perspective of things stressing their autonomous agency (Gibas et al. 2011, Bogost 2012, Grusin 2015).
- As cognitive. Katherine Hayles (2017) makes the argument that computational technology has cognitive capabilities that she describes as 'the cognitive nonconscious'. While it might not have a free will, she writes, it still has a choice and does make a decision in ever more spheres of our world.

As most of these different approaches above have been developed *before* the actual arrival of the internet of things, they seem to connect with a quality within things that has unfolded even more as things have become connected and learned to speak or to see. Informed by data, things learned to calculate decisions that fit our world, whereby they acquire a certain agency. Most certainly, to be connected to a network made things more independent from the human user – the human is now being served. Networked things can act without the user as they operate autonomously, informed by data. Before thinking that with this everything has been said, however, it is worth stopping for a moment, and looking critically at the autonomy things gain. For only at first glance do the theories that discuss a general agency of things listed above seem to have prepared us for the very specific agency of the internet of things. When we take a closer look, it becomes apparent that the thingness and the autonomy of connected things might be of a very different kind. What kind of *autonomy* or *agency* is it we are facing here? Do things gain autonomy and become 'smart', or are they just less dependent on their user? What kind of agency do things gain when a skill like seeing is applied to them? Let's return to self-driving vehicles and their accidents with this question and the concerns voiced above on our slightly worried minds.

The hypothesis that is to be tested here is simple: if cars truly gain agency, it will be the non-humans and not the humans that are to blame when something goes wrong. In search of an answer we return one more time to the approach of Critical Discourse Analysis and two company answers dealing with self-driving car accidents. Both, analysed below one after the other, are situated in the same context: they were released on the websites of Tesla and Google after accidents involving their self-driving cars, and belong to a genre mixture of PR text and explanatory blog post. Although they are discussing different aspects of those incidents, we study the texts to understand how they present the role of the car – the non-human – and its relation to its driver or its producer. Which position is seen as having agency?

Accident 1

When responding to the death of Joshua Brown, Tesla wrote:

> Neither Autopilot nor the driver noticed the white side of the tractor trailer against a brightly lit sky, so the brake was not applied. The high ride height of the trailer combined with its positioning across the road and the extremely rare circumstances of the impact caused the Model S to pass under the trailer, with the bottom of the trailer impacting the windshield of the Model S. Had the Model S impacted the front or rear of the trailer, even at high speed, its advanced crash safety system would likely have prevented serious injury as it has in numerous other similar incidents. (Tesla 2016b)

The first sentence of this paragraph centres around two active subjects, *autopilot* and *driver*. Both are linked to an action, which they did not perform – they did not *notice*. The effect of their non-action, *the brake was not applied*, is presented as a conditional clause manifesting their relation. But with the second slightly longer additive sentence that follows, the perspective fundamentally changes. While car and driver were active subjects in the first sentence, they are not any more in the second. Instead, the car finds itself as a passive object: something *caused* it to *pass under the trailer*. Here, the circumstances become the active subject: *height of trailer, positioning, rare circumstances of impact* have an effect on the car – it is no longer the car which acts or has agency. If the circumstances change, which is the aspect discussed in the third sentence, then the car can become active again; it would be likely to be able to control or at least influence the conditions it faces; it would *have prevented serious injury*.

To a certain extent one could say that by addressing the car as active and passive, by listing driver and car, which did not *notice*, as well as circumstances as causes for the crash, the text applies an actor-network theory approach. The autopilot, the driver, the height of the trailer, its positioning across the road and the brightly lit sky come together in a network of human and non-human things. Note that in the last sentence the driver does not get mentioned any more. One can safely assume that if the driver had paid attention, he would have also been able to influence the outcome of this situation, and it is interesting that this aspect isn't stated. Maybe because it shifts the blame to the driver, or maybe because then Tesla would have questioned its very own business: on its autopilot web page it announces for the car 'full self-driving capability at a safety level substantially greater than that of a human driver'.

Accident 2

In its monthly reports, which were published on its website, Google commented on its incident as follows:

> We've now reviewed this incident (and thousands of variations on it) in our simulator in detail and made refinements to our software. Our cars will more deeply understand that buses and other large vehicles are less likely to yield to us than other types of vehicles, and we hope to handle situations like this more gracefully in the future. (Google Self-Driving Car Project 2016)

As with Tesla we find the position of an active subject changing over two sentences, although in a very different manner. In the first sentence, the personal pronoun *We* is clearly linked to the human actors employed by Google. The sentence is describing their action, which was to *review this incident*, a review that links to the second part of the sentence in a weak causal relation: *and made refinements to our software*. In the second sentence, the car becomes the subject, which *will more deeply understand*. The auxiliary verb *will*, however, diminishes the active role of the car, as does the possessive adjective *our*.

Looking at those analyses, one recognizes immediately that both accidents are argued very differently while having one pivotal aspect in common. For the text published by Google, of the relationship of the human actors (company) and the non-human actors (car) one could say the following: Google's car, even though it appears in only one sentence as an acting subject, has a performing position. The non-human (car) is executing advice that was given by the humans (company). Moving on from the accident, it is the company that is applying changes which the car then has to perform. The situation is clear: the car does not take the blame. The mistake was caused because the self-driving vehicle was programmed wrongly by *our software* in a similar manner to a parent taking the blame for something that *your child* broke. Indicating that it is *our* mistake, it is Google's team of engineers who promise to learn from the car's misbehaviour – as for the car, it will be made to *understand*.

The argument of Tesla is slightly different, and not only because the role of the company never gets discussed. Here both the human (driver) and the non-human (the car and other non-human factors such as the positioning of the trailer) are active subjects which play their part in the accident. And by presenting the car as linked to other circumstances in an actor-network fashion, the car escapes the blame. So although they argue differently – Tesla presenting the car, the driver and the situation they find themselves in as a network of actors; Google presenting their engineers coding a computer program as the cause for the car's performance – the car never takes the blame. And as accidents are generally situations in which agency comes to the fore, one could conclude that neither case provides evidence of a new autonomy of non-humans, and that despite driving themselves, the cars were not the ones to blame. Which leads us to the conclusion that computer vision might enable cars and other connected things to *act* in a more autonomous way, but that does not mean that they *are* autonomous – a difference important to notice. For computer programs have been engineered by humans and should therefore be held accountable – a point made by Susan Schuppli (2014, 2017) when discussing the difficulties we face when holding algorithms accountable in law. Even in machine learning and when computers figure out rules by looking at large amounts of data, machines can only teach themselves according to the material *humans show them*. Technology companies such as Tesla or Google might like to present computers as of another kind, and introduce them as the solution that should assist the faulty human, if it suits them. But they are also willing to put the blame on circumstances for which the engineer did not yet program the software. A closer look will always show that technology does not have fewer flaws than a human but instead *has very different ones*, as Cathy O'Neil (2016) pointed out in her remarkable analysis of big data increasing inequality. Nor does it automatically act in a more objective way, although it applies a very different perspective – wrongly, we assume software to be unbiased as it is simply crunching data. This is why the last part of this chapter looks at cases in which computer programs failed to see what clearly stood in front of them. What can be seen and what cannot be seen by computer vision can be flawed to a degree that reveals their vision to have inbuilt politics.

Inbuilt politics

When one is analysing the politics of media, the focus generally lies on media representation: that is, on how cultural representations produce and exchange meaning, from representations in the media of particular groups and communities to the ways that experiences or ideas are discussed (Hall 1997). Here, researchers look at how specific aspects of society get represented, at who is given a voice and who is being ignored. The same aspect needs to be considered when it comes to computer vision and networked things gaining the ability to see: whose reality gets technically assisted and whose gets ignored? What are the inbuilt politics? As we live more and more in technically assisted realities, it is important to understand who gets the help of technology and who is overlooked, as is the case in the following two examples.

Example 1

An early example of computer vision failing to see that attracted a lot of attention was the motion-tracking webcam that came with Hewlett-Packard's Media Smart computers. By measuring the contrast between eyes, cheek and nose, the face-tracking software of this computer caused the webcam to zoom in and follow a person when their face started to move – or at least if that face belonged to a white person. A YouTube video uploaded by users demonstrated how the webcam correctly tracks the movements of Wanda Zamen's white face as she sways in front of the screen. But the same camera would stop moving when her black co-worker Desi Cryer appeared in the frame. 'Nope, no face recognition anymore, buddy', commented Cryer in the video. After demonstrating the flaw for a couple of minutes his conclusion was clear: 'I'm going on record and I'm saying it. Hewlett-Packard computers are racist' (Zamen 2009). Hewlett-Packard blamed the problem on 'insufficient foreground lighting' (BBC News 2009). But this insufficient foreground lighting did not seem to cause a problem with white Wanda. In their quick reaction, HP promised to look into this issue and said its software was 'built on standard algorithms'. This is an interesting choice of words, suggesting that they did nothing unusual and therefore could not have done anything wrong. Still, those 'standard algorithms' had obviously been optimized for a particular set of people that were exactly supposed to be the standard: those with white skin.

Example 2

A very different problem occurred when a new Google Photo app feature was rolled out in 2015, which was quickly made popular by many users. It allowed users to store photos in the cloud, but also analysed and organized photos automatically by tagging them, identifying features such as beaches, skyscrapers, specific cities, bikes, or graduations. In its *people* category, it would also group together similar faces, which it proudly announced it could even identify by age. But when labelling photos of New York software developer Jacky Alcine, it made a fundamental mistake: it tagged photos of him and a black female friend not as people. They were labelled *gorillas*. Alcine (2015) took to Twitter, and Google immediately removed the gorilla tag from the app. Besides their apology, they discussed what went wrong. Alcine, being familiar with machine learning, suspected that the engineers had trained the computer on insufficient sample material, and questioned Google's engineers over the 'images and people [. . .] used in their initial priming that led to results like these' (BBC News 2015). But the tagging feature had also not been optimized for people with black skin. A Google spokesperson agreed and told BBC News (2015) that 'there is still clearly a lot of work to do with automatic image labelling'.

To adopt Cheryl Harris's argument about *whiteness as a property*, technologies of visibility that do not recognize black people 'enshrine the status quo as a neutral baseline, while masking the maintenance of white privilege and domination' (Harris 1993: 1715). Digital visual technologies optimized for white faces confirm that skin colour remains relevant in post-colonial digital times – networked artefacts do not only have politics (Winner 1986), but today they also perform these politics. This has been the case before in technological history. Simone Browne (2016) discusses this in depth in *Dark Matters: On the Surveillance of Blackness*. And in his book *White*, Richard Dyer explores how developments in photographic media and cinematic lighting have used the filming of the human face as the benchmark, but have taken the *white* face as the standard. Dyer describes experiments with lighting, aperture size, the chemistry of film stock and development times, observing that: 'all proceeded on the assumption that what had to be got right was the look of the white face' (1997: 90). He concludes that within the cinema industry 'photographing non-white people is typically construed as a problem' (1997: 89; see also Rettberg 2014). The incident that Jacky Alcine made public showed that the computer industry has perpetuated this failing. Alcine rightly pointed out the need to 'correct the image Silicon Valley companies have with inter-sectional diversity', asking them to ensure that the voices of minorities 'are heard and not muted' (BBC News 2015). It is probably safe to assume that neither HP nor Google deliberately programmed their visual systems to malfunction with black customers but they also did not make sure that the technology works for them. Both visual systems seemed to be better at identifying white faces than black faces. By not optimizing their visual technologies for black skin tones, they indirectly declared them irrelevant. In her sharp analysis of 'homophily', Wendy Chun (forthcoming) has discussed this tendency to look just after your own as a disaster for our contemporary society relying on networks that are only theoretically open. Now, as things learn to see, it is important to ensure that the failures of the past are not reprogrammed into the things that will make up our world in the future.

Conclusion

When we talk of *self-driving* cars or vehicles that drive in *auto*pilot, or when we suggest that things have learned to see *with their own eyes*, we speak of an agency that new developments in technology made possible and that is now programmed by humans. As more and more things become connected to information, things are imbued with a new kind of agency – and for this a self-driving car is just one example. Yet still, those things are not autonomous. As our social practice gets more and more negotiated in technology, as much in public places as in factories, this chapter demonstrates that the skills informing that practice have to be studied as they shape our social fabric. Self-driving cars and their accidents, as much as machine learning and computer vision which inform the seeing of things – all those developments discussed in this chapter connect indeed to approaches from studies of media and communication. To the same degree that media scholars critically analyse media representations, looking into how particular groups and communities are portrayed, or at what topics are getting coverage, the skills of the internet of things must be held accountable in the future. And in the same manner as media scholars study media operations, the decision-making processes of computer programs need to be critically observed, understood, explained and publicly discussed. Besides looking at *media representation* (that is, the ways in which the media *portray* particular groups, experiences and topics, and from which perspective), we now also have to study *media recognition* (that is, how technology assists particular groups, experiences and areas and with what intentions). The next chapter, analysing *Tracking things*, will continue to spell out this necessity of media critique.

5

Tracking things

David Trinidad was concerned about his wife Ivonne's health. They were both users of Fitbit health-tracking devices, and Ivonne's was showing some unusual readings. Trinidad's first thought was that the sensors in the device weren't working properly. But rather than chase customer service, he decided to try asking users of Reddit, the social media platform that brands itself 'the front page of the internet'. Reddit users organize discussions on areas of shared interest through forums called subreddits. Trinidad posted his concerns on the subreddit dedicated to all things Fitbit:

> My wifes fitbit is showing her heartbeat being consistently high over the last few days. 2 days ago, a somewhat normal day, she logged 10 hours in the fat burning zone, which i would think to be impossible based on her activity level. Also her calories burned do seem accurate. I would imagine if she was in the the fat burning zone she would burn a ton of calories, so its not lining up.
>
> Im not sure if something is wrong with the sensor. is there a way to reset or recalibrate the device? (Trinidad [YoungPTone] 2016)

A user with the screen name of 'Thatwasunpleasant' responded that those sensors' readings could have another explanation – Ivonne was pregnant. A doctor's test confirmed the diagnosis, and the couple went on to track the course of the pregnancy on Instagram as *babyfitbit*.

What is striking about this story is not that a random online stranger could identify signs of pregnancy from a scrappy description. What is striking is that this information is being mediated at all – equipped with sensors, the things around us have started to track the world around them, and this world includes us as objects to be tracked ourselves. Questions about one's partner's metabolism would once not have seemed obvious things to post on 'the front page of the internet'. And yet using internet of things devices to share personal health data with strangers is becoming increasingly normalized and accepted, whether those strangers present themselves as individuals with opaque screen names, or as apps and devices manufactured by major corporations. Thanks to the internet of things, the personal, the intimate, the pathological, are now all to be mediated, to be *shared*.

The technological underpinning for this comes from dedicated health-monitoring devices (such as the Fitbit), from apps designed to work with major platforms (such as Android), and from the increasing integration of health technologies and tracking sensors into smartphones. Apple's iPhones, for example, come with a built-in *Health* system that can track and collect a wide range of body measurements for use with third-party apps; these apps can be integrated into Apple's HealthKit application programming interface. It lists as defaults certain types of data that can be tracked and distributed, including: calorie counts; blood alcohol and glucose levels; data on vitamin, caffeine or carbohydrate intake; levels of calcium and copper, iron and zinc; how many steps you've taken, how many flights you've climbed, how many times you've fallen over. Apps can analyse your sleeping patterns or adjust your workout routine; they can set you a goal of how many glasses of water to drink each day and they may then trumpet the results to your friends. This is not information that has been mediated until now.

Of course, people have developed ways of tracking their personal health or changes in their bodies since long before sensing networks – diaries and personal logs or scrapbooks, for instance (Neff & Nafus 2016: 14). Leonardo da Vinci is credited with inventing an early pedometer more than 500 years ago (Brabazon 2015). A low-tech tracking example would be the pencil marks on a door-frame made by parents to record changes in their child's height (Lupton 2016: 29). And a simple bathroom scales is a tracking technology – and one that, as Nafus observes, can fuel anxiety, shame or guilt about one's own behaviour just as much as it may encourage new practices (2016: x). Such systems chime with those that Michel Foucault identified as 'technologies of the self'. For Foucault, these were one set of 'techniques that human beings use to understand themselves' (1988: 18):

> technologies of the self, which permit individuals to effect by their own means or with the help of others a certain number of operations on their own bodies and souls, thoughts, conduct, and way of being, so as to transform themselves in order to attain a certain state of happiness, purity, wisdom, perfection, or immortality. (Foucault 1988: 18)

Foucault offers examples including philosophical reflection, the exchange of personal letters, the keeping of diaries, the interpretation of dreams and participation in religious confessionals as techniques of self-knowledge. But the use of networked digital media to generate, record and circulate intimate health data is a qualitatively different experience from writing a dieting diary in a notebook. Thanks to the internet of things, what Foucault once described has now turned into a technology of the public self: internet of things devices are used not just to monitor but also to *circulate* information about one's folate levels or body mass index. While there is much excitement in the humanities and social sciences about the possibilities of so-called Big Data, size is not the only thing that matters. As well as the quantitative dimension of Big Data, there is also the qualitative dimension that health tracking raises for the individual user. These are *different* data creating a *different* self. As Sam McAuliffe (2017) states, instead of listening to our inner voice, we are finding ourselves studying the data that are our external reality.

To get a sense of how different, consider the technologies of this new self on offer for today's internet of things. There is the We-Vibe networked vibrator, controlled by a smartphone app. There are connected toothbrushes that film the inside of the user's mouth. There is First Response, which describes itself as 'the first & ONLY Bluetooth wireless technology enabled pregnancy test'. There is a smart trampoline that monitors your jumps. There is the Babypod wireless internal vaginal speaker that plays music to one's unborn baby while it is still *in utero*. There is a Bluetooth-paired basketball. There are the Minna devices for both men and women that invite the user to sync their internal exercising with an app and to 'play games using your pelvic floor muscles'. There is a connected swimming costume. There is a smart condom. There is the my.Flow Bluetooth menstruation tracker – a connected tampon that can alert its user when she needs a replacement. There is a skipping rope that syncs with an app. There is the

Bluetooth diaphragm that detects cervical dilation in women about to give birth. There are smart dumbbells.

This chapter is about the wearable health devices of sensing networks. It discusses the increasing integration of sensors and health surveillance technologies into networked things. It situates this in the historical context of the development of wearable technologies, showing the connections to established social media business models. This chapter concentrates on the case of Fitbit, a major manufacturer of tracking technologies, using a Critical Discourse Analysis approach to explore the power relationships revealed in the ways in which Fitbit communicates both to and about its users. It discusses how users are variously positioned as engaged in constant competition and monitoring – *playful surveillance* – while at the same time those users are engaged in producing personal, even intimate, data for what may be unimagined audiences.

Keeping watch

In 1945, Vannevar Bush published an article called 'As We May Think', which anticipated and directly influenced the development of many key features of the contemporary internet. This essay is often cited for its legendary speculation about the never-built *memex* device, and for its visionary anticipations of hypertext and collaborative computing. The same essay also looked ahead to voice-activated devices – direct antecedents of today's conversational technologies Siri or Alexa, which we discussed in chapter 3. But while the *memex* is the best-known aspect of 'As We May Think', it is less often observed that Bush also speculated in that essay about near futures for *wearable* computing and connected things. He described a head-mounted camera, with a built-in display included within an otherwise ordinary pair of glasses – a direct antecedent of Google Glass or Snapchat Spectacles. At a time when computers barely existed, Vannevar Bush already saw the potential for devices that were both networked and wearable. In this sense, ubiquitous networked objects have been anticipated for as long as ubiquitous networked computers, and wearable devices are among the earliest antecedents of today's internet of things.

For many years, wearable connected computers seemed to be little more than futurist vapourware. As with other aspects of the internet of things, wearables manifested a certain strain of celebratory hype about their potentials and possibilities, bubbling along on allusions to secret agents or *Star Trek* tech. Back in the mid-1990s, even as the nascent web was still becoming established as a domestic medium, *Wired* magazine columnist and MIT Media Lab director Nicholas Negroponte was already writing about a near future in which 'your right and left cufflinks or earrings may communicate with each other by low-orbiting satellites' (1995: 6). The very banality of this image, and the socio-economic class dimensions implied by those cufflinks, capture the limitations of many visions of wearable computing – satellite-enabled cufflinks are a perfect example of a solution in search of a problem.

The reverse of this celebratory hype was of course a more dystopian vision, in which ubiquitous computing connotes *inescapable* computing. This dystopian perspective connects with more thoughtful conceptions of the cyborg, the digital self, and the convergence of the technological with the biological, to which we will return at the end of this chapter. For now, we can note that as cyborg theorist Donna Haraway insists, 'We're inside of what we make, and it's inside of us' (interviewed in Kunzru 1997). Mamoru Oshii, director of the *anime* classic *Ghost in the Shell*, whose cyborg vision of enhanced and engineered networked bodies has been very influential on twenty-first-century cinema, expressed the dystopian vision of wearable computing very well when he told one interviewer that he declined to have an email address, a mobile phone, or even a watch:

> There is a very tiny difference between whether those tools are inside of your body or outside it. Really, it doesn't matter. You have already become part of the machine; you have become a device. (Oshii interviewed in Cameron 2004)

As Vannevar Bush's 1945 essay reminds us, experiments in combining computing devices with clothing, jewellery and eyewear, as well as with body modifications and implants, have surprisingly long histories. While wearable computing appeared to move from the prototypes lab to the high street with the 2014 launch of Google's Android Wear platform for smartwatches and the announcement of the Apple Watch, neither Google nor Apple was the first to launch a smartwatch – rudimentary wrist-mounted games machines and computing devices had been produced by other well-known watch, computer and phone brands for several decades. But the cultural cachet and commercial clout that Apple and Google bring to their products, as well as the integration of their software with their operating and payment platforms and software apps ecosystems, mean that the release of Android Wear and the Apple Watch marked a new level of domestication for wearable internet of things technologies. Networked computers can now be worn on, in or as clothing or accessories. Communication devices can be worn on the body. And wearable devices can be fitted with sensors (the Apple Watch includes sensors that monitor the user's heart rate). So the development of wearable devices is an important element of the media environment of sensing networks. And this wearable internet is the element of the internet of things that raises the most troubling questions of privacy and surveillance; of the circulation, ownership and visibility of intimate personal data.

A central figure in the development of wearable tech has been Canadian academic Steve Mann, who has been developing wearable devices since the 1970s and deploying these in activist and artistic projects. One example of his activist-art projects is the Griefcase – a briefcase with a fingerprint scanner that allows access for anyone at all *except* its actual owner; so security guards demanding access to the briefcase can do so only by themselves consenting to being fingerprinted (Mann 2014). Mann has published numerous articles documenting his work in developing more portable, less cumbersome and more discreet wearable devices that combine computing and communications systems with networked visual and recording technologies (a good introduction is Mann 2013).

In July 2012, Mann claimed to have been assaulted by staff at a McDonald's in Paris. In his account, several staff members objected to him wearing his self-invented, augmented-vision technology, and ripped the device from his head. In a blog post, he observed the many ironies of a corporation that itself deploys surveillance cameras on its premises objecting to a customer having analogous capacities. He also pointed to how the legitimate uses of networked camera technologies were themselves being incorporated into the marketing strategies of corporations like McDonald's: for example, shops encouraging the smartphone user to scan QR codes for promotions may very well also have signs forbidding the use of the same device's camera. So using a smartphone camera to translate a menu or magnify its text to make it easier to read could perhaps have been unacceptable for the staff Mann encountered in the incident he describes; but using the same device to scan QR codes to take part in marketing promotions would be encouraged, in a social paradox yet to be resolved.

This paradox prompted Mann to propose the concept of *McVeillance*, which he defines as: 'the installation or using of surveillance cameras while simultaneously prohibiting people from having or using their own cameras, hand-held magnifiers, smartphones, or the like' (Mann 2012). From this perspective, *surveillance (from above*, or as Mann points out, *oversight*) becomes the dominant mode of vision. At the same time, *sousveillance (from below*) is disallowed (on *sousveillant* systems, see Mathiesen 1997). This imbalance of power is expressed by Mann in a droll equation, in which the number of *surveillance systems* divided by the number of vision technologies used by those *under* surveillance equals the measure of *McVeillance*. 'A society with oversight-only', he notes, 'is an oversight on our part' (Mann 2012).

Mann's account of his alleged assault and his capturing of these trends as *McVeillance* point to some of the central dilemmas of networked technologies of visibility for the internet of things. Much of the emerging internet of things environment is, in Mann's terms, *oversight-only*. His Paris encounter was a precursor of the response that would be encountered by early adopters of Snapchat's augmented vision system Spectacles, or of Google's Glass (the latter withdrawn from distribution, at the time of writing, but still in development). The imbalances of power, the uncertain ethics of visibility, the lack of clear cultural or social norms, the unanswered question of *who benefits?*, and the sheer creepiness of such networked wearable visual technologies converge in an especially cautionary perspective on the internet of things.

Firm wear

If mediating personal health data has become more accepted and commonplace, this is in part because of the experience of social media platforms. Social media have done much to train users of internet of things devices to accept the disclosure of personal information as normal and routine. They demand ever more information about our behaviour, and demand ever more access to our personal and intimate information in an escalating cycle. If you install the Facebook app, for instance, it will request permission to do a surprising range of things: Facebook will want permission to edit your calendar and add events; to access your call history and call your contacts directly; and to read and modify that contacts list. Facebook will also want to read your texts, to use your device to take pictures and video, to record where you are, and to stop your phone going to sleep (Facebook, Inc. n.d., Share Lab 2015). All of this would have struck many people as outrageous just a few years ago, but is now part of the everyday fabric of networked digital media life. We now hand over access to these data as the price of access to the other people in our lives. This is the business model that is drawing software and digital device firms like Apple, Facebook, Google and Microsoft into the health-tracking sphere.

These major internet and social media firms are all moving into the health-tracking business in their own ways. Google has its Google Fit tracking system that users can customize to their preferred activities and extend into the Android app ecosystem. Facebook includes a whole 'Health & Wellbeing' section of 'Life Events' that users can record as part of filling in the boxes to build their template-driven timeline. Facebook's default set invites the user to list details of illnesses overcome, bones broken, weight lost, habits quit, and to share the details of their new glasses or contact lenses, or of their 'new eating habits'. Microsoft has its HealthVault platform for users to document and set access permissions for personal medical data. It also has its Microsoft Health application platform, and produced its now discontinued Microsoft Band wearable wrist tracker devices (we'll pause a moment here for the Microsoft user to make their own *blue screen of death* joke).

Fitness trackers are an important part of the environment of sensing networks. A tracker, whether worn on the wrist or in the pocket or clipped to one's clothing, is a networked package of sensors. The Microsoft Band range for example wraps a package of eleven sensors around its wearer's wrist: an optical heart rate sensor, a three-axis accelerometer/gyro, a gyrometer, GPS, an ambient light sensor, a skin temperature sensor, a UV sensor, a capacitive sensor, a galvanic skin response sensor, a microphone and a barometer. Each of these tracks and records different data about the wearer's metabolism and movements. Such trackers collect and then sync what can be very intimate health details with mobile or desktop apps through wireless networks.

The US company Fitbit, Inc. has been an important player in the field of health-based sensing networks. At the time of writing, Fitbit is the market leader in the sale of wearable networked fitness trackers, with yearly revenues totalling more than $2.16 billion (Fitbit, Inc. 2017: 35). IT industry analysts Gartner estimated that the worldwide wearable market for 2016 would reach sales of more than 274 million devices, generating almost $29 billion in revenues (Gartner, Inc. 2016). The first tracker produced by the Fitbit company was released in 2009; as of 2017, the company produces a range of ten wearable fitness-tracking devices, and a wireless-internet-enabled bathroom scales. Entry-level models, targeted at everyday users who want to increase their daily physical activity, can clip onto clothing or be worn on the wrist as a bracelet; more expensive models, some targeted at serious runners or gym-goers, others at athletes, include features that offer incoming call and text notifications and music streaming from the smartphone with which they are paired.

Each user creates a Fitbit account and uses the wearable tracker to sync their bodily data with a dashboard and apps on their computer or phone. There is a searchable database of more than 300,000 food items, whose calorific intakes can be logged by the user in their app to help them measure their physical activity and weight. The company's own software tracks a range of personal data: steps taken, floors climbed, distance covered; calories burned, heart rate, sleep quality and duration; weight, body fat, body mass index; there are GPS location-tracking features and a proprietary system that measures continuous movement in a range of sports and activities. In addition, Fitbit's application programming interface (API) enables users to connect their data with thousands of third-party apps (Fitbit, Inc. 2017).

In common with other leading tech companies, Fitbit declares that it has a *mission*, and expresses this in a mission statement:

'Our mission. Fitbit helps people lead healthier, more active lives by empowering them with data, inspiration, and guidance to reach their goals' (Fitbit, Inc. 2017: 2). The network tech industry mission statement has become a genre in its own right, with certain key features recurring across those of the leading firms: they present the company as a public good, offering help to its users, with no mention of its actually operating as a business; they promote themselves as the solution to problems that may not really exist; and they rely on certain abstractions, with key terms such as *share, connect, power* and *inspire* recurring from one mission statement to the next (Meikle 2016: 37–41). Fitbit's mission statement is a good example of the genre – *helps people, empowering, inspiration, guidance* – and as with others, it reveals a lot about the power relationships that are coming to characterize the internet of things for its users.

But Fitbit goes further than just a standard mission statement. Fitbit also has a published *manifesto*. This is an odd thing for a manufacturer of sports equipment. A manifesto is a declaration, a programme of promised change. It makes convictions public. It is a fundamentally radical genre, one that makes the case for the new. A manifesto may promise world-making or world-wrecking. There are towering historical precursors – the ninety-five theses of Martin Luther, the declarations of the American and French revolutions – but it is a particularly modern genre. From Marx and Engels onwards, the manifesto has been perhaps the most modernist of textual forms – taken up by feminist voices from Mina Loy to Valerie Solanas; in the announcements of artistic ruptures from Dada and the Surrealists, to the Situationist promise that 'We will wreck this world'; in the radical rejection of social orders by the Black Panthers or the Unabomber; and in the reimagining of the possibilities of art and society through the embrace of technological possibility, from Marinetti's Futurism to Donna Haraway's cyborg. How does the Fitbit manifesto fare in such company?

> On the walk to work, at the weight room or in the last mile.
> Somewhere between first tries and finish lines. Pillow fights and pushing limits. That's where you find fitness.
> Every moment matters and every bit makes a big impact. Because fitness is the sum of your life. That's the idea Fitbit was built on – that fitness is not just about gym time. It's all the time.

How you spend your day determines when you reach your goals. And seeing your progress helps you see what's possible.
Seek it, crave it, live it. (Fitbit, Inc. n.d.)

What kind of text is this, and what kind of person is the *you* that it addresses? And what does this tell us about the power relationships that are being established through the new networked health environment of the internet of things? Here we return again to some tools from Critical Discourse Analysis (CDA) to explore how meanings are suggested or created (Fairclough 2003, Machin & Mayr 2012, Hansen & Machin 2013). For this, we examine the Fitbit manifesto for its word choices and patterns, for its textual organization and assumptions, and for the use of image and design to contribute to the meanings of the text. The first thing to note is how many of the word choices are striking – the use of *bit*, to connote both *small piece* and *unit of digital information*; or the weird choice of *pillow fights* as a marker of physical activity, its connotations variously playful, youthful, perhaps erotic. The first three sentences are incomplete – they lack verbs, lack subjects – and work like a narrative hook, to get the reader's curiosity engaged before the fourth sentence introduces the topic of *fitness*. The word *fitness*, which appears three times, is actually quite abstract, as are many of the key words in the text, such as *goals, progress* or *what's possible*. The direct, second-person address puts the text in a position of authority, as do the many imperative verbs (*live it*). Most of the things that *you* are said to do are about desire or discovery (*you find, seek, crave*). And the unspecified *it* in that final trio of imperative verbs invites the reader to supply their own desires, and to pursue them hard (*crave it*).

Because fitness is the sum of your life. This is the pivotal sentence around which the whole text revolves. It is placed halfway through the text, acting as the conclusion to the first part of the manifesto, and as the premise for the second part, which uses it to justify Fitbit's business model (*That's the idea Fitbit was built on*). Think of the many meanings of that word *sum*, its use here brilliant in its multiple connotations. There is *sum* as a matter of money or worth, a calculation of value or cost. There is *sum* as a matter of arithmetic, an adding and subtracting, a *reckoning*. There is *sum* as a matter of essence or gist, as the upshot or conclusion. There is *sum* as a matter of final meanings, as when a speaker *sums up* their evidence and arguments. And the *Oxford English Dictionary* also lists, among many other senses of the word, an obsolete archaic sense (the *OED* offers two examples from Milton's *Paradise Lost*) in which *sum* is the '*ultimate end or goal; the highest attainable point*'.

What of the background image on which the written text is superimposed on Fitbit's website? In the left third of the picture, a young man, perhaps in his late twenties, is out for a run. He's running through a street, its brick walls, glimpses of scaffolding and fencing, and wire-covered windows suggesting the kind of redeveloped post-industrial area in which tech start-ups may locate. His bare, muscular arms accentuate the very large Fitbit prominently located on the side closest to the viewer. He is closed, intense, and doesn't look at the viewer, but past us, too focused on his goals to acknowledge anyone else. We are invited instead to observe his example. The overall suggestion is of serious business – dark tones, purposeful focus, a gritty background environment, all suggesting the need to train and be strong.

So this leading producer of tracking things markets itself in a particular way that positions the user as a competitive individual engaged in a continuous series of struggles and challenges, in which winning and achieving unspecified goals are all that count. It urges toughness, perseverance, focus, discipline. Its mission statement and manifesto offer a discourse, a way of seeing and speaking about the world that comes to represent that world, which overlaps completely with the neoliberal individual of the corporate business world. In this, it extends that corporate world view into one's leisure time and away-from-work activity. To track one's health through the internet of things is to position oneself within that world view. Even when away from the office, one has to be setting targets, monitoring performance and reaching milestones. Whether with oneself, one's partner or with networked strangers on some fitness app's leaderboard, one is expected at all times to *compete*.

Playful surveillance

To encourage such competition, Fitbit sends the user achievement badges as they reach certain milestones – a *Boat Shoe Badge* for walking 5,000 steps and making it look 'easy breezy'; a *Marathon* badge for having walked 26 miles since the tracker was first activated; and a *Great Barrier Reef* one, once that total reaches 1,600 miles. There is a *Skyscraper* badge for climbing 100 flights of steps in a day, and a *Shooting Star* badge for having climbed 20,000 floors since activating the device. This system of badges and notifications is both deeply trivial and weirdly profound. It positions the user's body as one more networked thing. There is also an optional competitive dimension to these activities, through social and motivational tools and through subscription-based online coaching services. In this way, the Fitbit turns its user's daily life into a game, in which they are challenged to beat their own or other people's high scores on activities such as walking, sleeping or resisting carbohydrates. This kind of competitive health tracking is an example of *gamification* – the often dubious use of gaming features within contexts that are not otherwise considered games (Bogost 2016). Such gaming features – tokens and rewards, challenges and badges, progress bars and level-ups, high scores and leaderboards – can encourage playful encounters with systems that might otherwise provoke mistrust or rejection, such as being invited to record and publicize one's resting heart rate or how many flights of steps one has climbed.

As Whitson (2013) points out, playing a game is a social act. Even if one is playing alone, the socially determined rules and structure of the game bring others into the picture. And as we experience the playing of games as something that is pleasurable because it involves other people, so the gamification of personal health care that gets further amplified by the internet of things leads us towards including other people in that frame too, sharing our individual metrics for purposes of competition or mutual support. As a result, we are drawn to sharing our personal information with others who we may not imagine or whose motives we may not know. The gaming elements are there to lead the user into responding to feedback and modifying their behaviour. In this analysis, gamification can be understood as a mechanism that 'applies playful frames to non-play spaces, leveraging surveillance to evoke behaviour change' (Whitson 2013: 164). This behaviour change is built upon coaxing the user to bring the device and its software into their personal care and development, and into their physical and emotional goals. At the same time, the user yields intimate information about that care and those goals to the database of the firm producing the device or the app. So the connected device also becomes a disciplinary mechanism, as the user is nagged to reach their programmed daily targets. Such extensions of gaming features can be seen as not only *playful*, but also as carefully directed *surveillance*.

One useful definition of surveillance is: 'the focused, systematic and routine attention to personal details for purposes of influence, management, protection or direction' (Lyon 2007: 14). In an ever increasing range of daily situations, individuals are subject to ever increasing monitoring, recording, inspection and scrutiny. From daily social media use to workplace performance management, from ubiquitous public cameras to the monitoring of the most mundane financial transactions, surveillance has become inescapable (Andrejevic 2012). And yet, for the most part, as leading surveillance scholars note, many people seem either happy or resigned to acquiesce in the exchange of personal visibility for claims of security or for access to services (Lyon et al. 2012). Such acquiescence can also be achieved through presenting surveillance as a game.

Digital surveillance is often conceptualized in terms of labour – 'the work of being watched', as one scholar has it (Andrejevic 2004: 97). But it can also be understood in terms of play. *Play* is, of course, a complex word. As Brian Sutton-Smith showed (1997) the word *play* can be mobilized in a number of very distinct discourses, several of which are relevant to a discussion of the gamification of personal health data. Most obviously, to talk of play can be to talk about self-fulfilment and recreation – the care and development of the self. It can also be to talk of learning and development, as in the sense through which children are encouraged to play as an aspect of education. But play can also be connected to discourses of power and performance, and to discourses of chance and risk. Each of these discourses intersects in the playful surveillance of fitness trackers. Digital games are built on algorithms that set the rules and govern the space of play. The process of playing a digital game is one of learning and applying its rules, eventually mastering its simulation of space (Frasca 2004, Bogost et al. 2011).

The health tracker badges are one defining part of the internet of things, with their rewards, leaderboards and high scores. They extend competition into new arenas of daily life, such as meeting targets for drinking glasses of water or for sleeping a specified number of hours. In the case of games built around one's own weight loss, daily step-count or heart rate, the question then becomes one of who sets the rules. If a game is a rule-bound system, then who determines the rules for one's play with fitness apps? What is the normative standard by which the player is judged? For example, a daily 10,000 steps might be too much for many people in many circumstances. But it is suggested as the default by the device – not just in a one-size-fits-all fashion, but also as a benchmark against which the users are to judge themselves for daily compliance or failure (Neff & Nafus 2016: 40). For some users, accepting the invitation to explore systems that have been set for them by others might mean that they find their performance fails to meet the presented normative standards of body image, size, or self-care. So to what extent might playing the game expose the player to feelings of shame or inadequacy for their own incompatibility with the standards encoded by the game's governing algorithms? An inability to meet the Fitbit's opening target of 10,000 steps a day may spur some users to a competitive response, but for other people may also damage their self-esteem, with counterproductive effects on their health. The gamification element of this kind of playful surveillance, then, is a game that the player can lose.

Data entry

From a medical point of view, tracking and evaluating specific health data can be useful – for example, when monitoring people with kidney problems, as has been tested in a collaboration between the NHS and the research company Deep Mind. This becomes worrying, however, when health becomes a question of performance. When data are used to control a user and to shape a user's behaviour more than to monitor health and assist the user, things change. A Fitbit turns its user's life into a kind of performance management system, a free-time extension of the corporate workplace of goals, reviews and key performance indicators (KPIs). The user's entire life is to be enacted in a kind of neoliberal gymscape, in which both sleeping and drinking glasses of water become target-driven KPIs, while sitting and walking become spreadsheet rows to be targeted and monitored, tracked and analysed. Fitbit offers *Group Health* programmes for companies, that are 'guaranteed to get your employees moving' (https://www.fitbit.com/uk/group-health). Employees are supplied with one of Fitbit's 'family of trackers', and are then enrolled in various kinds of company challenges, with their work administrators able to access activity data. Employees of BP, for example, are said by Fitbit to have taken more than 23 billion steps as part of its *wellness* programme. Retail giant Target offered Fitbit devices to all its 335,000 employees in its own corporate wellness exercise (Chen & Pettypiece 2015). Fitbit devices, the company states, are 'the fitness tracker employees love'. Perhaps so, but alongside that rather infantilizing claim is a screenshot of a graph depicting the kinds of information that employers are able to generate about their workers through Fitbit's programmes. This graph groups employees as *very active, active, lightly active* or *sedentary*. This is described as an example of 'the data you need to gather meaningful, valuable results about your wellness investment'. What might the implications of this be for the 3.8 per cent of employees in this example who are identified as *sedentary*? Or even the 42.3 per cent identified as only *lightly active*?

Fitness trackers as a specific genre of the internet of things make it possible for companies to enrol their employees in corporate 'wellness' programmes. Their growing use, however, can create anxieties for workers who may worry they cannot meet the benchmarks of the programme, and who may fear losing their jobs as a result. It can create pressure to use non-work time to meet the demands of the employer's programme's targets, calling into question the distinction between work hours and non-work hours (Neff & Nafus 2016: 28–31). In this, corporate 'wellness' initiatives illustrate what Melissa Gregg (2011) has called 'presence bleed' – the blurring of the distinction between work and non-work time, as digital technologies are deployed not only to enable but to actually require or demand employees' availability at all times. What's more, wearable health-tracker firms, including Fitbit, now partner not only with employers but also with insurance companies, in licensing the data generated about employees in corporate wellness programmes (Lupton 2016: 124). It is not difficult to see how the intimate data created in this perhaps coercive process could lead to individuals being charged higher premiums for health insurance or denied coverage altogether, or lead to loss of employment or promotion. Proposals in this area are already being floated publicly by policy-makers and health authorities. A UK report by the Demos think-tank proposed offering 'easier access to healthcare' for people with demonstrably healthier lifestyles (quoted in Rich & Miah 2016: 11). Several regional health authorities in the UK (including in London, Yorkshire and Devon) have introduced plans to delay surgical operations for up to a year or to restrict access to IVF treatments in cases where patients smoke or have a particular level of body mass index (BBC News 2014, Campbell 2016, Lydall 2017).

People may track their own health, activity and behaviour for a range of reasons – curiosity, investigation, an attempt to change, or to reach goals. They may do this for a short period or over many years (Lupton 2016, Neff & Nafus 2016). As with exploring medical problems, such self-tracking is conceptually distinct from being the object of surveillance by others. Still, there may be substantial difficulties in practice in keeping one's self-tracking data secure from such surveillance (Barcena et al. 2014). The intimate personal data produced by tracking devices manifest very human aspects of each individual's life. Those data circulate through digital networks. They are mediated messages, whose subject may be unsure to whom they are addressed. As Lupton puts it, data 'have their own social lives, which are quite independent of the humans who originally generated them' (2016: 5). Moreover, as Nafus observes, data are only ever a *partial* representation of an individual human being (2016: 2). There is a risk that these partial representations, constructed by algorithmic choices, come to reduce that individual to their level. We are more than our data, but may be judged as though we were not. And the social lives of digital data produced through the internet of things can have significant consequences for the health, income or employment prospects of those human beings.

Gary Wolf and Kevin Kelly are co-founders of the *Quantified Self* (QS) movement. Wolf describes this as a 'loosely organized affiliation of self-trackers and toolmakers who meet regularly to talk about what we are learning from our own data' (2016: 67). From its first meeting in California in 2008, this QS movement has grown to more than a hundred groups with many thousands of participants who gather for presentations and workshops on self-tracking. Researchers, tech developers and enthusiasts share observations on their own self-tracking, framed around the themes 'What did you do, how did you do it, and what did you learn?' (Wolf 2016: 67). QS emphasizes the first-person experiences of the unique individual, rather than the impersonal aggregate, focusing on the $n=1$ sample size of the single user. In this way, Wolf suggests, QS can counter or 'slow down' the Big Data algorithms of state and corporate disciplinary medical infrastructures, whether these are internally focused on medicine and psychology or externally focused on behaviour and surveillance (2016: 72). But, in part, this is wishful thinking. In the same essay, Wolf offers the example of ankle bracelets placed on prisoners and parolees to monitor and constrain their behaviour. He writes that these devices can be traced back to an innovation originally intended to provide young offenders with positive feedback that would reduce their chances of reoffending. This, he writes, was the 'very first electronic life-logging device, a radio-signal-transmitting personal beacon' (2016: 71). So in the trajectory from a device that identified certain experiences as behaviours to be monitored to a device that constrains and disciplines users' choices and freedoms, Wolf observes a cautionary tale for today's internet of things.

The distinction between self-tracking and tracking by others is fundamental. Nissenbaum and Patterson (2016) point out that there are a range of different mechanisms through which personal health data may be distributed, and that these 'transmission principles' need to be factored into any discussion of the ethics of health tracking. For example, they note that a condition of using a Fitbit device is that the user consents to the data that it collects about their physical activity being uploaded to Fitbit's servers. This, they observe, is quite different from an individual's self-recording of their calorie or alcohol intake in a personal diary. Important variables include whether the circulation of personal data is voluntary or mandatory, is manual or automatic, and to what extent such data are to be shared further by others. In cases where employers receive information about their workers' personal health, questions of consent and of the ethical boundaries of work and life become ever more pressing (Nissenbaum & Patterson 2016).

Here it becomes useful to address the complex term *Big Data*. Big Data are often conceptualized in terms of size, or volume. So from this perspective, what makes Big Data big is that they're big. But that clearly isn't very helpful. It doesn't really capture the dynamics of the shifts in production, distribution, circulation and interpretation of data that are taking place. The many dimensions of information that are captured in this term are brought together in this impressive summary by Rob Kitchin, which is worth quoting in full:

> Big data are the outcome of the development and convergence of a range of technological advances in computing since the end of the Second World War. These include the production of mainframe computers in the 1950s and 60s; the nascent Internet in the 1970s and 80s that linked such computers together; the wide-scale roll-out of personal computers in the 1980s and 90s; the massive growth of the Internet in the 1990s and the development of Web-based industries, alongside a huge growth in mobile phones and digital devices such as games consoles and digital cameras; the development of mobile, distributed and cloud computing and Web 2.0 in the 2000s; the roll-out of ubiquitous and pervasive computing in the 2010s. Throughout this period a number of transformative effects took place: computational power grew exponentially; devices were networked together; more and more aspects and processes of everyday life became mediated by digital systems; data became ever more indexical and machine-readable; and data storage expanded and became distributed. (Kitchin 2014: 80–1)

Kitchin offers a nuanced taxonomy of characteristics of Big Data. First, yes, Big Data are enormous in size or *volume*. But second, they also have very high *velocity*, which is to say that they are created in real time, and third, they very diverse in *variety*. Big Data are also *exhaustive*, aiming for sample sizes of 100 per cent (where the Quantified Self mantra of *n=1* meets the Big Data ambition of *n=all*). Kitchin writes that Big Data are also very granular in *resolution* (level of detail) and *indexicality* (capacity to identify a unique individual). And they are able to be combined easily with other datasets because they are *relational* (sharing common fields), *flexible* (new fields can be added) and *scalable* up to new sizes (Kitchin 2014: 67–79). The size of the data, then, is only one aspect of why Big Data matter.

The convergence of the elements identified here by Kitchin as 'transformative effects' have been major drivers of the development of the internet of things. More powerful, more networked, more pervasive computing devices enable both more personally identifiable and automatically produced data, to be stored and processed in more elaborate infrastructures (often those proprietary corporate infrastructures that are masked by the childlike term *the cloud* [Mosco 2014]). This convergence makes possible the creation, distribution and processing of Big Data. These data may be *directed, automated* or *volunteered* (Kitchin 2014: 87). Directed data are those associated with familiar mechanisms of surveillance, monitoring and governance by human agents (passports, social security numbers, census forms, tax returns, school and medical records). Automated data are produced and may also be processed by digital systems operating on algorithms. For example, when a surveillance camera records your car's registration plate as you enter a toll road, or a public transport network such as that of London tracks the movements of its millions of daily users. Vast quantities of automated data are also produced by networked sensors in objects, and by the movements of users of cards with embedded chips (workplace or campus ID cards, shop loyalty cards, credit cards). Volunteered data are offered in a transaction or as a gift by users – contributions to social media, the yielding of personal information to surveys and consumer loyalty programmes, or participation in collaborative ventures such as Wikipedia (Kitchin 2014). Personal health tracking can involve the creation of *automated* data, if one authorizes a third-party app to collect, store and process certain intimate personal information generated by the sensors on a fitness-tracking device. It can involve the creation of *volunteered* data, when users choose to purchase a tracking device and select the options that they want to have tracked. And it can involve the creation of *directed* data, if an employee is required by their boss to wear a fitness tracker and participate in a corporate health programme.

More dangerous is that one's data are only as secure as the least secure node in the networks with which users share the data. Above all, the third-party apps that use the health APIs of the Fitbit or the iPhone or Android may not have the same exacting standards as the firms behind those devices and operating systems. Early research into the data-sharing practices of app producers has identified some disturbing findings:

> A study of twelve mobile health and fitness apps conducted by the U.S. Federal Trade Commission found that user data were disseminated to seventy-six third parties, and one app in particular sent data to eighteen other entities. [. . .] In addition to information, such as names, email addresses and usernames, twenty-two of those third parties received details on consumers, such as exercise information, meal and diet information, gender and geo-location. [. . .]. A similar study by web analytics and privacy group Evidon commissioned by the Financial Times found that the twenty most popular health and fitness apps share information with almost seventy companies. In particular, MapMyRun was found to transmit data to eleven companies, some of which were advertising firms [. . .] . (Till 2014: 449)

Fitbit formally partners with around forty different app companies, and thousands of other apps are also available for use with the device. Let's assume, for the sake of the argument, that every one of those companies now working with Fitbit has the most airtight privacy policy imaginable, that they hold their users' data as a sacred trust, and that those users have no reason to ever imagine anything could happen to their data. Let's assume further that every single person working at every single one of those companies is completely ethical, trustworthy and a safe person to entrust with intimate health data. But even under these ideal conditions, who will own those data in ten years' time? After all, companies fail, companies change hands, companies are bought out and stripped of their assets. So what could be the personal consequences for users if the company that owns the app with whom they share their most intimate health data is bought by the same firm that supplies them with health insurance?

If this sounds like paranoid speculation, consider the ongoing commercial value of Myspace. To many, this social media platform is only of historical interest, with its brief prominence in the middle of the first decade of the twenty-first century now long eclipsed by larger networks such as Facebook. Yet Myspace continues to change hands for eight-figure sums because its decade-old archive of user data remains valuable to advertisers – those data prompted Time, Inc. to purchase the owner of Myspace, a company called Viant, in 2016 (Jackson 2016). More than a decade after many users last logged into Myspace, the digital traces they left behind – contacts and connections, likes and dislikes, emotions and opinions – still offer lucrative data. In this context, the future trajectories of the personal health data that users of internet of things tracking technologies share with so many unknowable third parties are at best uneasy.

To look at the privacy policies published by Fitbit's partner apps is to see just how uneasy. For example, Fitstar, owned by Fitbit, makes the following assurance about 'Information shared with our partners':

> We share Personal Information with our parent company, Fitbit, to provide you with a comprehensive fitness experience. We also share Personal Information with entities that perform functions necessary to provide the Services. (Fitstar 2015)

The word *entities* there is on the vague side. With the above Myspace example in mind, the following disclaimer is also noteworthy:

> In some cases, we may choose to buy or sell assets. In these types of transactions, user information is typically one of the transferred business assets. Moreover, if we, or substantially all of our assets, were acquired, or if we go out of business or enter bankruptcy, user information would be one of the assets that is transferred or acquired by a third party. (Fitstar 2015)

Such language recurs throughout the privacy policies of the other firms whose apps are promoted as partners by Fitbit; almost all of these firms are third-party companies. In the main, the language of their privacy policies may be boiler-plate template phrases; but their very vagueness should make any user stop and think about what specific conditions could later apply – perhaps especially in relation to what kind of *entities* might *acquire* the app's *assets*, as these assets may include a substantial record of that user's personal health history.

A further concern for the user of networked health technologies is the potential for leaks of their data. In the wake of the Snowden revelations about state agencies' systematic intrusion into the data of digital media users, Apple and others have moved to strengthen the encryption protocols on their devices and software services. However, as Lupton points out (2016: 130), Apple still pushes users to implement its iCloud storage system, which has been the subject of high-profile breaches and hacks, such as those of female celebrities' private nude photos (Meikle 2016: 96–106). Breaches, hacks and leaks are not incidental to digital media. Rather, they are a central characteristic of digital networks. They are, in Paul Virilio's sense, an *accident* of the internet. Virilio has observed that every technological development also introduces its own distinct kind of accident: 'The invention of the airplane was the invention of the plane crash' (Virilio & Lotringer 1983: 32). Leaks are an intrinsic, fundamental feature of networked computing. A computer is a copying machine. The internet is a network of copying machines on which communication is a process of making copies of information sent between machines. If we email you a document, you then have a copy but we still have our own copy too, and traces may also remain on the servers through which our message passed on its way to you. Information multiplies as it moves from one machine to another, from server to laptop, from tablet to flash drive. Leaks are not only inevitable, but are fundamental to the internet.

Conclusion

The internet of things developments discussed in this chapter – wearable tracking technologies and the complex, intimate data that they create – push the quantification of the self and the technologizing of the body further. In doing so, they connect with discourses of the *cyborg* that have circulated across the humanities and social sciences for decades. Some of these discourses, such as Donna Haraway's famous manifesto for cyborgs, express optimistic visions of the possibilities of the convergence of the biological and the technological. Other visions of such convergence strike more cautionary notes. Below we contrast J. G. Ballard's novel *Crash* with Haraway's manifesto. These two texts stand as opposite poles on the terrain of imagining the technologizing of the body. We use them here to bring these perspectives to the health-tracking technologies of the internet of things, and their claims on the bodies of their users.

The word *cyborg* was coined in 1960 by researchers theorizing the demands of space travel (Clynes & Kline 1995 [1960]). Their cyborg was to be a self-regulating system that combined the biological and the technological, capable of interstellar voyages perhaps lasting thousands of years. But the word was given fresh currency in 1985, with the first publication of Donna Haraway's cyborg manifesto, a still dazzling essay that identifies multiple possibilities for working with the convergence of the technological and the biological. A cyborg, Haraway writes, is 'a hybrid of machine and organism, a creature of social reality as well as a creature of fiction' (1991: 149; see also Hayles 1995). Haraway's manifesto highlights the possibilities of blurred boundaries, such as those between the human and the technological. She celebrates 'rejoicing in the illegitimate fusions of animal and machine' (1991: 176). This embrace of the hybrid as a political model is to be a way beyond the reductive essentialisms of a concept like *nature* or *human*. As she writes in the famous last line of the essay: 'I would rather be a cyborg than a goddess' (1991: 181).

In some ways, Haraway's work anticipates the technological self-tracking of Fitbit users or of the Quantified Self movement. 'Communications technologies and biotechnologies are the crucial tools recrafting our bodies' (1991: 164). Both communications technologies and biotechnologies, Haraway argues, work in the same way: 'the translation of the world into a problem of coding' (1991: 164). Interviewed for *Wired* magazine, Haraway argued that one becomes conscious of oneself as a cyborg on turning up at the gym – packed with exercise machines and dietary supplements, a gym is a place that makes no sense without a cyborg concept of the body as machine. 'Think about the technology of sports footwear', she said. 'Before the [US] Civil War, right and left feet weren't even differentiated in shoe manufacture. Now we have a shoe for every activity.' Such specialization converges with 'the interaction of medicine, diet, training practices, clothing and equipment manufacture, visualization and timekeeping' (Haraway, quoted in Kunzru 1997). In this way, the self-tracking technologies of Fitbits and other digital health devices take this established model of cyborg self-design and extend it to the sensing, networked environment of the internet of things.

At the opposite end of the spectrum from Haraway's embrace of possibility stands J. G. Ballard's novel *Crash*. This astonishing book is one likely extreme of cyborg fantasy, with its dystopian vision of the 'marriage of sex and technology' (1973: 142). In *Crash*, the narrator recounts his friendship with Vaughan, a 'hoodlum scientist', who finds sexual fascination in both car crashes and their victims: 'In his mind Vaughan saw the whole world dying in a simultaneous automobile disaster, millions of vehicles hurled together in a terminal congress of spurting loins and engine coolant' (p. 16). As he grows dissatisfied with both non-fatal car crashes and non-fatal sex with their survivors, Vaughan plans his own death in an orgasmic vehicle collision with a car driven by the film star Elizabeth Taylor. Drawn ever deeper into Vaughan's fantasies and his efforts to make them real, which include stalking the narrator's wife for a trial run of the planned crash with the actress, Ballard's protagonist develops an absolute equivalence between the sexual and the technological: 'the true significance of the automobile crash, the meaning of whiplash injuries and roll-over, the ecstasies of head-on collisions' (p. 10). One sexual encounter in the back seat of a car is described as 'a dance of severely stylized postures that celebrated the design and electronics, speed and direction of an advanced kind of automobile' (p. 142).

For its author, *Crash* was a cautionary pornography about technology. He described porn as 'the most political form of fiction', because it is the genre most directly concerned with how people exploit each other (Ballard 1984: 98). Seen from this perspective, the anti-erotic technophilia of *Crash* becomes a political argument, and a useful one in thinking about the convergence of the biological and the technological that is captured in the hybrid metaphor of the cyborg. In his introduction to the French edition of *Crash*, Ballard observed: 'Science and technology multiply around us. To an increasing extent they dictate the languages in which we speak and think. Either we use those languages, or we remain mute' (Ballard 1984: 97). This is one way of imagining a politics of the internet of things. Between the visionary possibilities of Haraway's cyborg and the dystopian exploitations of Ballard's *Crash* are today's intimate, wearable, networked devices, and the commercial interests that fuel their development. As ever, the central question should be *who benefits?* The tracking things of the wearable internet demand both a politics and an ethics of mediated visibility. Sensing networks contribute to the shaping of an environment in which each of us may need to add our voice to debates about technological questions. As the internet of things extends around us – and at times within us – such a politics becomes more necessary than ever.

6
Last things

This book has explored the internet of things from a specific perspective: it has studied the shifting roles of things by looking at their newly acquired skills. By analysing how things locate, speak to, see and track the world around them, we discussed, chapter for chapter and skill for skill, what happens *when things become media*. Often the changes those things undergo seem simple – a matter of some small automation that adds some convenience. But one should make no mistake – once connected and able to communicate, things' roles in our world fundamentally change. Sensors generate and circulate information in ways that turn things into actors in networks of communication. And networked sensors mean that the sensed information can be compared with other data to calculate a response. As we explain in chapter 1, the networks that surround us have become *sensing networks*. The internet of things is changing our relationships with technology in all kinds of ways – these are not necessarily better or worse, but they *are* different.

The internet of things changes the status of objects – a networked object is different from the pre-networked version. Our relationships with our personal devices, for example, become intimate in new ways. A phone that talks to you is different from a phone that just lets you talk to other people, and it takes on a different role and status in its user's life. The internet of things changes the ownership relationship between individuals and the networked devices that produce and circulate data about them – at the same time that your Alexa device is working for you, it is also working for Amazon. The networked device, already the repository for so many of our thoughts, activities and connections with others, also produces and circulates information about us. Its sensors track our locations and movements, its barometer monitoring the atmosphere around us, its microphone recording the soundscape we move through. With the conversational devices of sensing networks, technology becomes *a dialogue partner*. We move from caressing our touch-screen phones to whispering to our conversational technologies. The use of voice interfaces such as Siri or Alexa increases, and the graphical user interface that had come to seem the natural way of interacting with computers is now revealed as contingent – an aspect we discuss in detail in chapter 3. This new dialogue partner is always available to talk, but also always to listen – and perhaps also to record and remember.

The internet of things initiates the discussion of the agency of technologies anew – *some agency, no intention*, as we put it in chapter 1. To understand the politics of this agency is important, because internet of things systems might reduce or increase but surely will *change* the agency of the individual user. For example, it becomes more difficult to make meaningful choices about one's engagement with networked technologies if those technologies are dispersed across the entire environment through which we move, work and live. Before the internet of things, we might offer up data about ourselves as we click *like* and *share* on our friends' latest pictures, or as we hand over our credit cards and supermarket loyalty cards. But now, from sensors in street lights that we drive past, to the conversational technologies in the background listening for their wake word, data about each person's daily life are generated about them without their choosing to log in or create a profile. How does one opt out of such a situation? If the surveillance business model of social media becomes distributed across the environment, it is much more difficult to find an alternative. Users of Facebook or Gmail who are concerned about the collection of their personal information can elect to deactivate their accounts. But people living in a networked city, surrounded by connected devices and sensors, have fewer such options. For them, data are not just something they choose to give but something that they give off, as their movements, purchases, activities and interactions are recorded and circulated by myriad sensing networks.

A primary concern of media and communication scholars has always been the production and interpretation of messages and texts. These interpretations have variously been seen as created by individual speakers or authors, or by audiences, or through a collaborative process of the making of meaning. But in an internet of things environment, meaning is no longer produced only by speakers or authors, and the very meaning of *audiences* shifts yet again. Instead, the making of meanings is now a dispersed process that also involves networked sensors and linked databases. In this sense, messages and texts take on a new status. They are no longer merely the expression of human thought and behaviour, but are also produced by algorithms and data – we look into examples of this production in chapters 4 and 5. That meaning has technical aspects is of course nothing new. Technology has always been profoundly involved in the exchange of communication and meaning (Derrida 1997); and it has been so most explicitly in the digital age, in which network technology is constantly assisting us with exchanging our messages (Brunton 2013, Chun 2016: 52), and as computer protocols establish a connection from one end of the internet to another. But this kind of machine-to-machine communication was generally there to assist us – to ensure that the computer at the other end was connected to the network, or that our servers could identify the numerical address of a domain, or that spam messages would be filtered out. In other words, such machine-to-machine communication served the human activity of communication, which was still the most important element that all other aspects of communication centred around. So far. With the internet of things, this partly changes. Connected things talk to us directly, thereby adopting the position of a human dialogue partner, and for this they locate us, record us, see on our behalf, process our information, and communicate *about* us. And this fundamentally transforms formerly familiar parameters of communication: for example, by opening up dialogues to multidirectional conversations among a variety of actors.

A major aspect of the study of media has long been questions of representation. Media have often been critically analysed for the ways in which they portray particular groups and experiences, and from whose perspective. For the internet of things, the question of representation needs to be adjusted in two ways:

1. Sensing networks communicate data *about* certain groups, and we need to ask in whose interests and to what effects also in regard to policies. Which groups are targeted and for what reasons? Can

evaluated data be accessed and controlled by the user, or do they only serve the interests of the company? And last but not least, are they safe? These questions are explored in chapter 5 using the example of fitness trackers.

2. Sensing networks also *recognize* certain groups better than others. The internet of things creates technology that *assists the reality of some people better than that of others.* So with the internet of things, next to the question of *media representation*, the question of *media recognition* becomes central and should inform policies. Whose reality is to be assisted by sensing networks and whose experiences are to be left unrecognized? For which particular group is a system created and with what intentions? In chapter 4, we discussed recognition systems that fail to recognize black users, as those systems have not been optimized for them.

The internet of things matters because it changes the fabric of our daily lives. For example, the surveillance issues that are part of health-tracking technologies, conversational devices or technologies of networked visibility are as transformative as the privacy issues we faced before with social media. In both cases, social media and the internet of things, it is important to separate the communicative affordances of a system from the individual firms or technologies that have delivered them. Even if Facebook and Twitter were both to disappear overnight, the changes in daily communication they introduced would persist in new contexts: both of those social media platforms have encouraged and enabled a convergence of public and personal communication which would continue to be expressed in other systems even if they went away. Facebook and Twitter have made natural the new ways in which public communication takes on a personal quality. The convergence of public and personal is one aspect of social media that has become sufficiently ubiquitous and normalized that it would likely persist beyond the lifespan of any one social media firm, however dominant they may seem at present: the social media repertoire with its self-selected networks – the tags and likes, the follows and shares – is now a fundamental part of daily mediated communication.

In a similar way, the affordances of the internet of things are also becoming part of the fabric of daily digital life, in the normalization of conversational technology devices, of health-tracking systems, or of cars that resemble laptops with wheels. As with social media, hundreds of millions of connected individuals have come to take for granted the capacities of their always-on, location-aware, networked sensing devices. It now already feels natural that the small object in our hand can sense its environment and tell us where we are and how to get to the station, even if we ourselves have no clue. It feels natural that the device can listen to the song playing on the cafe radio and link us directly to the artist's web page. It feels natural that the device is where and how we record ever more intimate details of our calorie intake and sleeping pattern, our daily step-count and resting heart rate. It feels natural that when we speak to the device it speaks back. This addressed device that speaks to, sees and tracks its user represents a set of fundamental shifts in our experience of mediated communication. And these shifts are becoming dispersed across the wider environment, as the capabilities of the smartphone are given to cars, to light bulbs and to TV sets. The smartphone is the most accessible example, but it is only one example of how networked sensors and connected things are being given new capacities to communicate with and about us.

Here the reader might object that this shift isn't one affecting all of us. As we emphasize internet of things devices that already exist, it might seem that this book is populated by expensive objects only affordable to some of us, by self-driving cars and surveillance systems, by the health concerns of the affluent, and by the domestic choices of those able to purchase novelty devices. The Fridge Fallacy of chapter 1 would have it that the internet of things is still largely a phenomenon of the middle class. Some readers may suggest that our choices of emphasis in this book align with that fallacy. But companies are beginning to subsidize the take-up of connected technologies in order to get at more people's data. While the $3,000 networked fridge is likely to remain a niche purchase, connected shopping buttons embedded around the house have lower barriers to usage. It may not be long before conversational technologies move from dedicated objects like the Echo or the iPhone to become ubiquitous features of connected things. Each individual's personal data, after all, are valuable enough for many different kinds of actor to offer him or her new ways to yield their data up.

There are some signs that the challenges we face with the internet of things are being taken up by regulators and policy-makers, who have so far largely deferred to market mechanisms. One key initiative has been the European Union's General Data Protection Regulation (GDPR – for an overview see http://www.eugdpr.org). The GDPR is intended to ensure that businesses which engage with EU individuals' personal data adhere to certain principles about how they handle those data, and it threatens enormous fines for companies in breach of its data protection principles. But there are still massive challenges in implementing data protection principles in practice, to say nothing of the hundreds of millions of internet of things devices already in use, and not all firms will have the resources to easily build in 'privacy by design' into their internet of things systems. The emphasis in the GDPR on software providers is an important reminder that security in this context is not just about protecting users from hackers, but also from firms that may gather their personal data in unexpected or unethical ways.

There is also a very real need for security standards that would prevent the hacking and hijacking of connected devices. Tiny connected things – a toaster or a car key – might seem as though they do not need to be made secure against the intrusions of even the most elementary hacker. But we should recall the example of the *Mirai* botnet – discussed in chapter 2 – which was able to recruit a vast swarm of TVs and printers in a coordinated assault on one key part of internet architecture. A related issue was revealed by the global diffusion of the WannaCry ransomware in May 2017, which saw the files on hundreds of thousands of computers encrypted against their owners' wills, and which caused major disruption to the UK National Health Service. The ransomware exploited older Windows operating systems for which Microsoft no longer offered support or security updates. In the context of the internet of things, for how long will the manufacturers of networked digital objects offer security support? The lifespan of a domestic fridge may be ten or fifteen years – will the operating system on a networked one continue to receive software support for so long?

A further obstacle to regulation is that internet cultures have long had a libertarian streak that sees government and regulation as not only undesirable but as impossible in a networked environment. This view found its most indelible impression in John Perry Barlow's 'Declaration of the Independence of Cyberspace' (1996). For Barlow, governments were 'weary giants of flesh and steel' who were to have no sovereignty in 'the new home of Mind' that was the internet. More than two decades on, this seems, at worst, reactionary rhetoric, or, at best, wishful thinking. To call for an unregulated internet is one thing when it is about fostering free speech and a space for the untrammelled expression of opinion. It would be quite another when it is about allowing the unsecured connection of any kind of object to networks of surveillance and data-mining, vulnerable to weaponized swarms.

As surveillance becomes networked and dispersed – a matter of networked sensors and machine communication, not just of Facebook or CCTV – so its data become ever more indexical, relational, granular. So, for all of these reasons, there should be privacy recommendations or standards that act as one mechanism for regulating the development of sensing networks. These may involve legal standards, market mechanisms, technological affordances, user rights or the emergence of new social norms – most likely, all five. Such privacy standards might reach back to the foundational modern view of privacy as 'the right to be let alone' (Warren & Brandeis 1890) – an expansion perhaps of the European 'right to be forgotten' into the 'right to be left unmonitored'. Perhaps 'privacy by design' should mean that connected sensing devices come with a mandatory opt-out switch that stops their data being circulated beyond the device itself. Perhaps 'flight mode' will become something that individuals can choose to enter in daily life, not just something that applies to their phones. Leaks would still occur – they are, as we suggested in chapter 5, intrinsic to the internet itself – but the user would have at least the possibility of minimizing their own exposure with each device.

But this would become much harder as soon as a person leaves their house – and the connected public transport card takes them onto a train or bus that is filled with other people's conversational technologies and visibility devices, and that moves them through an environment where sensors locate and track on scales of unimaginable complexity. As that person moves from the train or bus through the supermarket and the office, the movements and pauses, every tiny thing that catches their attention, all feed further linked databases for analysis and interpretation. What privacy standards could apply here? What mechanisms of opt-out and self-care – what technologies of the self – can be deployed when the cloud becomes the daily weather?

Here, we would suggest that new social norms will continue to develop around our relationships with internet of things technologies. There has been a reductive emphasis on productivity and the economy in too much discussion about the internet of things. How will the social norms around internet of things devices change as these become more ubiquitous? Will it be acceptable to have Alexa listening to your party or Siri scanning the conversation on your date? Will one need to ask all passengers if they are OK with the car going on autopilot? How can employees exercise meaningful choice if their employer requires them to wear health-tracking technologies at all times, and what kinds of support or recourse can they seek if they choose not to wear them? In chapter 5 we invoked Paul Virilio's (1983) observation that every technology produces its own accident. Benjamin Bratton (2015) has extended Virilio's idea to point out that accidents also produce technologies. The invention of the car produced the new kind of accident that is the car crash, but that accident in turn produced the new technology of the airbag. The accidental visibility and surveillance industries of twenty-first-century digital media have produced in turn technologies that privilege the anonymous and the ephemeral – Virtual Private Network (VPN) systems, the Tor network, or the fleeting interactions of Snapchat as a reaction to the eternalized entries on Facebook. *What will be the Snapchat of the internet of things?* What will be produced in response to the accidents of sensing networks in order to promote the ephemeral, the removable, the impermanent? It is not hard to imagine ever more necessary *obfuscation*: 'the deliberate addition of ambiguous, confusing, or misleading information to interfere with surveillance and data collection' (Brunton & Nissenbaum 2015: 1). Those authors' strategies of obfuscation – false echoes, misleading signals, loud noise, hidden locations, fake tells, collective identities, discarded devices, and many others – suggest future practices of everyday life through which people may offer tiny tactical replies to the ceaseless demands for data.

As a final observation, we will note that some of the most central and enduring questions in the study of media have been around production and ownership. Here it becomes useful to compare how such questions are different in relation to different models of mediated communication – the broadcast model, the social media model, and the internet of things model. In the *broadcast* model, the media industries produce and circulate texts – stories and songs, ideas and images, information and entertainment; in turn, their *audiences* produce their presence and attention, and their demographic attributes in a generalized, aggregate form. In the *social media* model, the media industries provide a platform infrastructure; in turn, their *users* produce the content, as well as their presence and attention, and their demographic attributes at both the aggregate level and the micro-targeted individual level.

But in the *internet of things*, an environment in which sensing and computing are ubiquitous and embedded, *humans themselves* become the text that is produced and circulated. Here, every gesture and movement, every purchase and heartbeat, every left-turn and wake word becomes a message for analysis, interpretation, exegesis and judgement. Who is the owner of these messages? Are they produced by the technological systems installed by particular people who may then claim property rights on the information created by their systems? Or are these part of the daily fabric of existence of the individuals whose personal data are captured for analysis simply by walking down the street? And do governments need to look into policies to ensure that some of those data stay open – such as transport or medical data – or will at least be available after an embargo? As ever, the key question becomes *who benefits?* For the internet of things, this is a question that each reader should answer for themselves. We hope that this book provides some guidance towards finding an answer.

References

5-Star Open Data (2015) 5 star open data, 31 August, <http://5stardata.info/en>, accessed 10 February 2017.

Abbate, J. (2000) *Inventing the Internet*. Cambridge, MA: MIT Press.

Alcine, J. (2015) 'Google Photos, y'all fucked up. My friend's not a gorilla', *Twitter*, 28 June, <https://twitter.com/jackyalcine/status/615329515909156865>, accessed 26 January 2017.

Allen, M. (2013) 'What was Web 2.0? Versions as the dominant mode of internet history', *New Media & Society*, vol. 15, no. 2, pp. 260–75.

Amodei, D., Olah, C., Steinhardt, J., Christiano, P., Schulman, J. & Mané, D. (2016) 'Concrete problems in AI safety', <https://arxiv.org/abs/1606.06565>, accessed 26 January 2017.

Anderson, B. (1991) *Imagined Communities* (revised edition). London: Verso.

Andrejevic, M. (2004) *Reality TV*. Lanham, MD: Rowman & Littlefield.

Andrejevic, M. (2012) 'Ubiquitous surveillance', in K. Ball, K. D. Haggerty & D. Lyon (eds.) *The Routledge Handbook of Surveillance Studies*. London: Routledge, pp. 91–8.

Andrejevic, M. & Burdon, M. (2015) 'Defining the sensor society', *Television and New Media*, vol. 16, no. 1, pp. 19–36.

Apple, Inc. (2016a) 'About Error 53', 13 September, <https://support.apple.com/en-us/HT205628>, accessed 1 January 2017.

Apple, Inc. (2016b) *Form 10-K (Annual Report)*, <http://investor.apple.com/financials.cfm>, accessed 29 September 2016.

Apple, Inc. (2016c) 'About iBeacon on your iPhone, iPad, and iPod touch', 30 June, <https://support.apple.com/en-gb/HT202880>, accessed 20 February 2017.

Arendt, H. (1998) *The Human Condition*. Chicago: University of Chicago Press.

Aristotle (1992) *The Politics*. London: Penguin.

Ashton, K. (2009) 'That "internet of things" thing', *RFID Journal*, <http://www.rfidjournal.com/articles/view?4986>, accessed 19 July 2016.

Ballard, J. G. (1973) *Crash*. London: Vintage.

Ballard, J. G. (1984) 'Introduction to *Crash*, French edition', in *RE/SEARCH #8/9 J. G. Ballard*. San Francisco: Re/Search, pp. 96–8.

Barbrook, R. & Cameron, A. (2015) *The Internet Revolution*. Amsterdam: Institute of Network Cultures.

Barcena, M. B., Wueest, C. & Lau, H. (2014) 'How safe is your quantified self?', *Symantec Security Response*, <https://www.symantec.com/content/dam/symantec/docs/white-papers/how-safe-is-your-quantified-self-en.pdf>, accessed 8 October 2016.

Barlow, J. P. (1996) 'A declaration of the independence of cyberspace', *Electronic Frontier Foundation*, <https://projects.eff.org/~barlow/Declaration-Final.html>, accessed 30 January 2017.

Barthes, R. (1981) *Camera Lucida*. London: Vintage.

BBC News (2009) 'HP camera "can't see" black faces', 24 December, <http://news.bbc.co.uk/2/hi/technology/8429634.stm>, accessed 15 December 2016.

BBC News (2014) 'NHS Devon surgery restriction for smokers and obese plan revealed', 3 December, <http://www.bbc.co.uk/news/uk-england-devon-30318546>, accessed 23 January 2017.

BBC News (2015) 'Google apologises for Photos app's racist blunder', 1 July, <http://www.bbc.com/news/technology-33347866>, accessed 15 December 2016.

Beck, A. & Hopkins, M. (2015) *Developments in Retail Mobile Scanning Technologies* [report]. Leicester: Department of Criminology, University of Leicester.

Beckett, S. (1983) *Worstward Ho*. New York: Grove Press.

Blackmore, J. (2014) 'Is Apple's iBeacon at risk of a tragedy of the commons?', *The Guardian*, 2 May, <https://www.theguardian.com/media-network/2014/may/02/ibeacons-tragedy-commons-marketers>, accessed 20 February 2017.

Bogost, I. (2012) *Alien Phenomenology, or, What it's Like to be a Thing*. Minneapolis, MN: University of Minnesota Press.

Bogost, I. (2016) 'Why gamification is bullshit', in W. H. K. Chun & A. W. Fisher with T. W. Keenan (eds.) *New Media, Old Media* (2nd edition). New York: Routledge, pp. 678–88.

Bogost, I., Ferrari, S. & Schweizer, B. (2011) 'Newsgames: An introduction', in G. Meikle & G. Redden (eds.) *News Online*. Basingstoke: Palgrave Macmillan, pp. 84–98.

Bolukbasi, T., Chang, K.-W., Zou, J., Saligrama, V. & Kalai, A (2016) 'Man is to computer programmer as woman is to homemaker? Debiasing word embeddings', <https://arxiv.org/abs/1607.06520>, accessed 26 January 2017.

Bordewijk, J. L. & van Kaam, B. (1986) 'Towards a new classification of tele-information services', *Intermedia*, vol. 14, no. 1, pp. 16–21.

Bostrom, N. (2014) *Superintelligence*. Oxford: Oxford University Press.

Brabazon, T. (2015) 'Digital fitness: Self-monitored fitness and the commodification of movement', *Communication, Politics & Culture*, vol. 48, no. 2, pp. 1–23.

Bratton, B. H. (2015) *The Stack*. Cambridge, MA: MIT Press.

Bratton, B. H. (2016) 'Can the bot speak? The paranoid voice in conversational UI', in R. Bishop, K. Gansing, J. Parikka & E. Wilk (eds.) *Across & Beyond: A Transmediale Reader on Post-digital Practices, Concepts, and Institutions*. Berlin: Sternberg Press, pp. 306–24.

Bria, F. (2016) 'The people's roadmap towards technological sovereignty tech for the common good participate @BCN_digital #BCNdigital http://ajuntament.barcelona.cat/estrategiadigital/ca', *Twitter*, 20 November, <https://twitter.com/francesca_bria/status/800355619903569920>, accessed 14 February 2017.

Bria, F., Sestini, F., Gasco, M., Baeck, P., Halpin, H., Almirall, E. & Kresin, F. (2015) 'Growing a digital social innovation ecosystem for Europe: DSI final report', European Union, <https://www.nesta.org.uk/sites/default/files/dsireport.pdf>, accessed 10 February 2017.

Bright, P. (2016) 'Tay, the neo-Nazi millennial chatbot, gets autopsied', *Ars Technica*, 26 March, <http://arstechnica.com/information-technology/2016/03/tay-the-neo-nazi-millennial-chatbot-gets-autopsied>, accessed 25 January 2017.

Brown, B. (2001) 'Thing theory', *Critical Inquiry*, vol. 28, no. 1, pp. 1–22.

Brown, B. (ed.) (2004) *Things*. Chicago: University of Chicago Press.

Brown, B. (2015) *Other Things*. Chicago: University of Chicago Press.

Browne, S. (2016) *Dark Matters*. Durham, NC: Duke University Press.

Brunton, F. (2013) *Spam*. Cambridge, MA: MIT Press.

Brunton, F. (forthcoming) 'Hello from Earth', *Communication*. Lüneburg: Meson Press.

Brunton, F. & Nissenbaum, H. (2015) *Obfuscation*. Cambridge, MA: MIT Press.

Bunz, M. (2014) *The Silent Revolution*. Basingstoke: Palgrave Macmillan.

Bunz, M. (2015) 'School will never end: On infantilization in digital environments – amplifying empowerment or propagating stupidity?', in D. Berry & M. Dieter (eds.) *Postdigital Aesthetics*. Basingstoke: Palgrave Macmillan, pp. 191–202.

Bunz, M. (2016) 'Things are not to blame: Technical agency and thing theory in the age of internet of things', in W. H. K. Chun & A. W. Fisher with T. W. Keenan (eds.) *New Media, Old Media* (2nd edition). New York: Routledge, pp. 388–400.

Burke, D. (2008) 'Google Mobile app for iPhone now with Voice Search and My Location', *Google Mobile Blog*, 17 November, <http://googlemobile.blogspot.co.uk/2008/11/google-mobile-app-for-iphone-now-with.html>, accessed 25 January 2017.

Bush, V. (1945) 'As we may think', *Atlantic Monthly*, July, <http://www.theatlantic.com/magazine/archive/1945/07/as-we-may-think/303881>, accessed 13 May 2017.

Cameron, D. (2004) 'Animation nation', *Sydney Morning Herald*, 22 October, <http://www.smh.com.au/news/Film/Animation-nation/2004/10/22/1098316838583.html>, accessed 12 July 2016.

Campbell, D. (2016) 'Surgeons attack plans to delay treatment to obese patients and smokers', *The Guardian*, 29 November, <https://www.theguardian.com/society/2016/nov/29/surgeons-nhs-delay-treatment-obese-patients-smokers-york>, accessed 9 January 2017.

Carey, J. (1989) *Communication as Culture*. New York: Routledge.

Carter, C. (2014) 'Shoppers steal billions through self service tills', *The Telegraph*, 29 January, <http://www.telegraph.co.uk/finance/personalfinance/household-bills/10603984/Shoppers-steal-billions-through-self-service-tills.html>, accessed 11 November 2016.

Castells, M. (2000) *The Rise of the Network Society* (2nd edition). Oxford: Blackwell.

Castells, M. (2001) *The Internet Galaxy*. Oxford: Oxford University Press.

Castells, M. (2004) *The Power of Identity* (2nd edition). Oxford: Blackwell.

Castells, M. (2009) *Communication Power*. Oxford: Oxford University Press.

Castells, M. (2012) *Networks of Outrage and Hope*. Cambridge: Polity.

CBS New York (2015) 'Seen at 11: Cyber spies could target your child through a baby monitor', *CBS New York*, 21 April, <http://newyork.cbslocal.com/2015/04/21/seen-at-11-cyber-spies-could-target-your-child-through-a-baby-monitor/>, accessed 14 February 2017.

Charniak, E. (1996) *Statistical Language Learning*. Cambridge, MA: MIT Press.

Chen, B. X. (2016) 'Siri, Alexa and other virtual assistants put to the test', *New York Times*, 27 January, <http://www.nytimes.com/2016/01/28/technology/personaltech/siri-alexa-and-other-virtual-assistants-put-to-the-test.html>, accessed 11 November 2016.

Chen, C. & Pettypiece, S. (2015) 'Target to offer Fitbits to 335,000 employees', *Bloomberg Technology*, 16 September, <https://www.bloomberg.com/news/articles/2015-09-15/target-to-offer-health-tracking-fitbits-to-335-000-employees>, accessed 26 January 2017.

Chun, W. H. K. (2016) *Updating to Remain the Same*. Cambridge, MA: MIT Press.

Chun, W. H. K. (forthcoming) *Pattern Discrimination*. Lüneburg: Meson.

Clynes, M. E. & Kline, N. S. (1995 [1960]) 'Cyborgs in space', in C. H. Gray with H. J. Figueroa-Sarriera & S. Mentor (eds.) *The Cyborg Handbook*. New York: Routledge, pp. 29–33.

Cohen, M. H., Giangola, J. P. & Balogh, J. (2004) *Voice User Interface Design*. Boston: Addison-Wesley Professional.

Coleman, G. (2014) *Hacker, Hoaxer, Whistleblower, Spy*. London: Verso.

Cowan, R. S. (1985) 'How the refrigerator got its hum', in D. MacKenzie & J. Wajcman (eds.) *The Social Shaping of Technology*. Milton Keynes: Open University Press, pp. 202–18.

Critical Art Ensemble (1994) *The Electronic Disturbance*. New York: Autonomedia.

Critical Art Ensemble (1995) *Electronic Civil Disobedience and Other Unpopular Ideas*. New York: Autonomedia.

Dale, A. (2016) 'Google displays wrong window from wrong country', *Tom's Hardware*, 28 May, <http://www.tomshardware.co.uk/answers/id-3072204/google-displays-wrong-window-wrong-country.html>, accessed 14 February 2017.

Daston, L. (2007) 'Things that talk', in L. Daston (ed.) *Things that Talk*. Cambridge, MA: MIT Press, pp. 9–26.

Dayan, D. (2009) 'Sharing and showing: Television as monstration', *Annals of the American Academy of Political and Social Science*, September, vol. 625, pp. 19–31.

Deleuze, G. (1995) *Negotiations*. New York: Columbia University Press.

De Mar, C. (2015) 'Baby monitor hacker sends a frightening message to Indianapolis family', *Fox 59*, 1 October, <http://fox59.com/2015/08/27/baby-monitor-hacker-sends-a-frightening-message-to-indianapolis-family>, accessed 20 February 2017.

Deng, J., Dong, W., Socher, R., Li, L.-J., Li, K. & Fei-Fei, L. (2009) 'ImageNet: A large-scale hierarchical image database', *Imagenet*, <http://www.image-net.org/papers/imagenet_cvpr09.pdf>, accessed 26 January 2017.

Denning, D. (2001) 'Cyberwarriors: Activists and terrorists turn to cyberspace', *Harvard International Review*, vol. 23, no. 2, pp. 70–5.

Derrida, J. (1997) *Of Grammatology*. Baltimore, MD: Johns Hopkins University Press.

Dhanjani, N. (2015) *Abusing the Internet of Things*. Sebastopol, CA: O'Reilly Media.

Dobuzinskis, A. (2016) 'Microsoft apologizes for offensive tirade by its "chatbot"', *Reuters*, 26 March, <http://www.reuters.com/article/us-microsoft-twitter-bot-idUSKCN0WS00D>, accessed 25 January 2017.

Doyle, G. (2013) *Understanding Media Economics* (2nd edition). London: Sage.

Dyer, R. (1997) *White*. London: Routledge.

El-Baz, A., Elnakib, A., Abou El-Ghar, M., Gimel'farb, G., Falk, R. & Farag, A. (2013) 'Automatic detection of 2D and 3D lung nodules in chest spiral CT scans', *International Journal of Biomedical Imaging*, <https://www.hindawi.com/journals/ijbi/2013/517632>, accessed 26 January 2017.

Ellul, J. (1964) *The Technological Society*. New York: Vintage.

Enge, E. (2014) 'The great knowledge box showdown: Google Now vs. Siri vs. Cortana', *Stone Temple Consulting*, 7 October, <https://www.stonetemple.com/great-knowledge-box-showdown/#VoiceStudyResults>, accessed 25 January 2017.

European Commission (2016) 'Advancing the internet of things in Europe', <http://eur-lex.europa.eu/legal-content/EN/TXT/?uri=CELEX:52016SC0110>, accessed 21 May 2017.

Evans, D. (2011) 'The Internet of Things: How the next evolution of the Internet is changing everything', *Cisco Internet Business Solutions Group*, <http://www.cisco.com/web/about/ac79/docs/innov/IoT_IBSG_0411FINAL.pdf>, accessed 20 January 2017.

Facebook, Inc. (n.d.) 'Why is the Facebook app requesting permission to access features on my Android?', *Facebook Help Centre*, <https://www.facebook.com/help/210676372433246>, accessed 29 March 2017.

Fairclough, N. (2003) *Analysing Discourse*. London: Routledge.

Ferguson, N. (2016) 'Tay, Trump, and artificial stupidity', *Boston Globe*, 3 April, <https://www.bostonglobe.com/opinion/2016/04/03/tay-trump-and-artificial-stupidity/9Zk3dP7CSByV5bzbc3L2vJ/story.html>, accessed 25 January 2017.

Fitbit, Inc. (2017) *Form 10-K (Annual Report)*, <https://investor.fitbit.com/financials/sec-filings>, accessed 29 March 2017.

Fitbit, Inc. (n.d.) 'Read our manifesto', <https://www.fitbit.com/uk/whyfitbit>, accessed 9 January 2017.

Fitstar (2015) 'Privacy policy', *Fitstar*, 22 July, <http://fitstar.com/privacy-policy>, accessed 26 January 2017.

Foote, A. (2015) 'Google Maps needs to have a "walking-but-not-walking-through-a-poorly-lit-sketchy-park-at-night-walking" directions feature', *Twitter*, 4 September, <https://twitter.com/amkfoote/status/640000521953259520>, accessed 16 February 2017.

fotoboy (2016) 'Amazon Alexa gone wild! (original)', *YouTube*, 29 December, <https://www.youtube.com/watch?v=r5p0gqCIEa8>, accessed 16 February 2017.

Foucault, M. (1977) *Discipline and Punish*. Harmondsworth: Penguin.

Foucault, M. (1980) 'The eye of power', in C. Gordon (ed.) *Power/Knowledge*. Brighton: Harvester Press, pp. 146–65.

Foucault, M. (1988) 'Technologies of the self', in L. H. Martin, H. Gutman & P. H. Hutton (eds.) *Technologies of the Self*. Amherst, MA: University of Massachusetts Press, pp. 16–49.

Franceschi-Bicchierai, L. (2017a) 'Internet of Things teddy bear leaked 2 million parent and kids message recordings', *Motherboard*, 27 February, <https://motherboard.vice.com/en_us/article/internet-of-things-teddy-bear-leaked-2-million-parent-and-kids-message-recordings>, accessed 29 March 2017.

Franceschi-Bicchierai, L. (2017b) 'How this Internet of Things stuffed animal can be remotely turned into a spy device', *Motherboard*, 28 February, <https://motherboard.vice.com/en_us/article/how-this-internet-of-things-teddy-bear-can-be-remotely-turned-into-a-spy-device>, accessed 29 March 2017.

Frasca, G. (2004) 'Videogames of the oppressed: Critical thinking, education, tolerance, and other trivial issues', in P. Harrigan & N. Wardrip-Fruin (eds.) *First Person*. Cambridge, MA: MIT Press, pp. 85–94.

Freak, J. & Holloway, S. (2012) 'How not to get to Straddie', *Redland City Bulletin*, 15 March, <http://www.redlandcitybulletin.com.au/story/104929/how-not-to-get-to-straddie>, accessed 13 November 2016.

Frith, J. (2015) *Smartphones as Locative Media*. Cambridge: Polity.

Gabrys, J. (2016) *Program Earth*. Minneapolis, MN: University of Minnesota Press.

Gartner, Inc. (2016) 'Gartner says worldwide wearable devices sales to grow 18.4 percent in 2016', 2 February, <http://www.gartner.com/newsroom/id/3198018>, accessed 8 October 2016.

Gartner, Inc. (2017) 'Gartner says 8.4 billion connected "things" will be in use in 2017, up 31 percent from 2016', 7 February, <http://www.gartner.com/newsroom/id/3598917>, accessed 20 March 2017.

Gell, A. (1998) *Art and Agency*. Oxford: Oxford University Press.

Gibas, P., Pauknerová, K. & Stella, M. (2011) *Non-Humans in Social Science*. Prague: Pavel Mervart.

Godwin, M. (1994) 'Meme, counter-meme', *Wired*, 2.10, <http://archive.wired.com/wired/archive/2.10/godwin.if.html>, accessed 10 June 2016.

Goggin, G. (2013) 'Changing media with mobiles', in J. Hartley, J. Burgess & A. Bruns (eds.) *A Companion to New Media Dynamics*. Malden, MA: John Wiley, pp. 193–208.

Goldsmith, J. & Wu, T. (2006) *Who Controls the Internet?* New York: Oxford University Press.

Google Self-Driving Car Project (2016) 'Monthly report', February, <https://www.google.com/selfdrivingcar/files/reports/report-0216.pdf>, accessed 15 December 2016.

Government Office for Science (UK) (2014) 'The Internet of Things: Making the most of the second digital revolution', <https://www.gov.uk/government/publications/internet-of-things-blackett-review>, accessed 17 September 2016.

Graham, M. (2014) 'Manuel Castells managed to write a sentence that includes the word "network" seven times!', *Twitter*, 17 December, <https://twitter.com/geoplace/status/545233614049669121>, accessed 17 January 2017.

Grandis, K. (2012) 'Militarizing your backyard with Python: Computer vision and the squirrel hordes', *Pycon*, Santa Clara, <http://www.slideshare.net/kgrandis/pycon-2012-militarizing-your-backyard-computer-vision-and-the-squirrel-hordes>, accessed 26 January 2017.

Granovetter, M. (1973) 'The strength of weak ties', *American Journal of Sociology*, vol. 78, no. 6, pp. 1360–80.

Greengard, S. (2015) *The Internet of Things*. Cambridge, MA: MIT Press.

Gregg, M. (2011) *Work's Intimacy*. Cambridge: Polity.

GreyB (2014) 'Google driverless car – The obstacle detection unit', *The Future of Technology*, 14 June, <https://greybmusings.wordpress.com/2014/06/14/google-driverless-car-the-obstacle-detection-unit/>, accessed 28 January 2017.

Gross, D. (2013) 'Foul-mouthed hacker hijacks baby's monitor', *CNN*, 14 August, <http://edition.cnn.com/2013/08/14/tech/web/hacked-baby-monitor>, accessed 20 February 2017.

Grusin, R. A. (2015) *The Nonhuman Turn*. Minneapolis, MN: University of Minnesota Press.

Hall, S. (ed.) (1997) *Representation*. London: Sage.

Hannon, C. (2016) 'Gender and status in voice user interfaces', *Interactions*, vol. 23, no. 3, pp. 34–7.

Hansen, A. & Machin, D. (2013) *Media and Communication Research Methods*. Basingstoke: Palgrave Macmillan.

Haraway, D. J. (1991) *Simians, Cyborgs, and Women*. London: Free Association Books.

Haraway, D. J. (2008) *When Species Meet*. Minneapolis, MN: University of Minnesota Press.

Harris, C. (1993) 'Whiteness as property', *Harvard Law Review*, vol. 106, no. 8, pp. 1707–91.

Hauser, M. D., Chomsky, N. & Fitch, W. T. (2002) 'The faculty of language: What is it, who has it, and how did it evolve?', *Science*, vol. 298, no. 5598, pp. 1569–79.

Hayles, N. K. (1995) 'The life cycle of cyborgs: Writing the posthuman', in C. H. Gray with H. J. Figueroa-Sarriera & S. Mentor (eds.) *The Cyborg Handbook*. New York: Routledge, pp. 321–35.

Hayles, N. K. (2009) 'RFID: Human agency and meaning in information-intensive environments', *Theory, Culture & Society*, vol. 26, nos. 2–3, pp. 47–72.

Hayles, N. K. (2017) *Unthought: The Power of the Cognitive Nonconscious.* Chicago, IL: University of Chicago Press.

Heidegger, M. (2001) 'The thing', in *Poetry, Language, Thought*, translated by A. Hofstadter. New York: Harper & Row, pp. 161–84.

Hern, A. (2014) 'What is Apple's iBeacon?', *The Guardian*, 13 January, <https://www.theguardian.com/technology/2014/jan/13/what-is-apple-ibeacon-retail-tracking>, accessed 20 February 2017.

Hird, J. (2010) 'Ten horrifying display ad placements', *Econsultancy*, 1 October, <https://econsultancy.com/blog/6666-ten-horrifying-display-ad-placements-nsfw>, accessed 16 February 2017.

Hirschberg, J. & Manning, C. D. (2015) 'Advances in natural language processing', *Science*, vol. 349, no. 6245, pp. 261–6.

Hodder, I. (2012) *Entangled*. Chichester: Wiley-Blackwell.

Howard, P. N. (2015) *Pax Technica*. New Haven, CT: Yale University Press.

Hu, T. H. (2015) *A Prehistory of the Cloud*. Cambridge, MA: MIT Press.

Hunt, E. (2016) 'Tay, Microsoft's AI chatbot, gets a crash course in racism from Twitter', *The Guardian*, 24 March, <https://www.theguardian.com/technology/2016/mar/24/tay-microsofts-ai-chatbot-gets-a-crash-course-in-racism-from-twitter>, accessed 26 January 2017.

Hutchins, J. (1995) ' "The whisky was invisible" or persistent myths of MT', *MT News International*, no. 11, pp. 17–18.

Huxtable, L. (2012) 'This bs Google Maps be sending me on some rapey-town mission. All thru the park at night when the place is across the street. Smh', *Twitter*, 20 October, <https://twitter.com/BrooklynBettyB/status/259834046455095296>, accessed 16 February 2017.

Ingold, T. (2010) 'Bringing things to life: Creative entanglements in a world of materials', *Realities Working Paper #15*, ESRC National Centre for Research Methods, University of Manchester.

Jackson, J. (2016) 'Time Inc buys what is left of MySpace for its user data', *The Guardian*, 11 February, <https://www.theguardian.com/media/2016/feb/11/time-inc-buys-what-is-left-of-myspace-for-its-user-data>, accessed 9 January 2017.

Kalantar-zadeh, K. (2013) *Sensors: An Introductory Course*. New York: Springer.

Karpathy, A. (2014) 'What I learned from competing against a ConvNet on ImageNet', *Andrej Karpathy Blog*, 24 January, <http://karpathy.github.io/2014/09/02/what-i-learned-from-competing-against-a-convnet-on-imagenet>, accessed 26 January 2017.

Karpathy, A. (2015) 'The unreasonable effectiveness of recurrent neural

networks', *Andrej Karpathy Blog*, 21 May, <http://karpathy.github.
io/2015/05/21/rm-effectiveness>, accessed 26 January 2017.

Karpathy, A. (n.d.) 'Multimodal recurrent neural network', <http://
cs.stanford.edu/people/karpathy/deepimagesent>, accessed 26 January
2017.

Karpathy, A. & Fei-Fei, L. (2015) 'Deep visual-semantic alignments for
generating image descriptions', *Proceedings of the IEEE Conference on
Computer Vision and Pattern Recognition*, pp. 3128–37.

Kelly, K. (2011) *What Technology Wants*. New York: Viking.

Kirksey, K. (2005) *Computer Factoids*. Lincoln, NE: iUniverse.

Kitchin, R. (2014) *The Data Revolution*. London: Sage.

Kittler, F. (1999) *Gramophone, Film, Typewriter*. Stanford, CA: Stanford
University Press.

Krizhevsky, A., Sutskever, I. & Hinton, G. E. (2012) 'ImageNet classification
with deep convolutional neural networks', *Advances in Neural Information
Processing Systems*, pp. 1097–1105.

Kung, S. Y. & Taur, J. S. (1995) 'Decision-based neural networks with signal/
image classification applications', *IEEE Transactions on Neural Networks*,
vol. 6, no. 1, pp. 170–81.

Kunzru, H. (1997) 'You are cyborg', *Wired*, 5.02, February, <http://www.
wired.com/1997/02/ffharaway>, accessed 12 July 2016.

Laboria Cuboniks (2015) 'XF XENOFEMINISM: A politics for alienation',
<http://www.laboriacuboniks.net/>, accessed 16 February 2017.

Latour, B. (1991) 'Technology is society made durable', in J. Law (ed.) *A
Sociology of Monsters*. London: Routledge, pp. 103–31.

Latour, B. (1992) 'Where are the missing masses? The sociology of a few
mundane artifacts', in W. Bijker & J. Law (eds.) *Shaping Technology/
Building Society*. Cambridge, MA: MIT Press, pp. 225–58.

Latour, B. (1993) *We Have Never Been Modern*. New York: Harvester
Wheatsheaf.

Latour, B. (2000) 'The Berlin key or how to do words with things', in P.
Graves-Brown (ed.) *Matter, Materiality and Modern Culture*. London:
Routledge, pp. 10–20.

Latour, B. (2005) *Reassembling the Social*. New York: Oxford University Press.

Leiner, B. M., Cerf, V. G., Clark, D. D., Kahn, R. E., Kleinrock, L., Lynch, D.
C., Postel, J., Roberts, L. G. & Wolff, S. (2000) 'A brief history of the
internet', *Internet Society*, <http://www.isoc.org/internet/history/brief.
shtml>, accessed 8 July 2016.

Levin, S. & Woolf, N. (2016) 'Tesla driver killed while using autopilot
was watching Harry Potter, witness says', *The Guardian*, 1 July,
<https://www.theguardian.com/technology/2016/jul/01/

tesla-driver-killed-autopilot-self-driving-car-harry-potter>, accessed 15 December 2016.

Lupton, D. (2016) *The Quantified Self*. Cambridge: Polity.

Lydall, R. (2017) 'Smokers and obese Londoners could be refused surgery in bid to save NHS cash', *Evening Standard*, 10 January, <http://www. standard.co.uk/news/health/smokers-and-obese-londoners-could-be-refused-surgery-in-bid-to-save-nhs-cash-a3436771.html>, accessed 23 January 2017.

Lyon, D. (2007) *Surveillance Studies*. Cambridge: Polity.

Lyon, D., Haggerty, K. D. & Ball, K. (2012) 'Introducing surveillance studies', in K. Ball, K. D. Haggerty & D. Lyon (eds.) *The Routledge Handbook of Surveillance Studies*. London: Routledge, pp. 1–11.

Machin, D. & Mayr, A. (2012) *How to do Critical Discourse Analysis*. London: Sage.

MacKenzie, D. & Wajcman, J. (eds.) (1999) *The Social Shaping of Technology* (2nd edition). Buckingham: Open University Press.

Madden, M. & Rainie, L. (2015) 'Americans' attitudes about privacy, security and surveillance – report', *Pew Research Center*, 20 May, <http://www. pewinternet.org/2015/05/20/americans-attitudes-about-privacy-security-and-surveillance>, accessed 26 January 2017.

Mann, S. (2012) 'McVeillance: How McDonaldized surveillance creates a monopoly on sight that chills AR and smartphone development', *Steve Mann's Blog*, 10 October, <http://eyetap.blogspot.co.uk/2012/10/mcveillance-mcdonaldized-surveillance.html>, accessed 14 July 2016.

Mann, S. (2013) 'Wearable computing', in M. Soegaard & R. F. Dam (eds.) *The Encyclopedia of Human-Computer Interaction* (2nd edition), <https:// www.interaction-design.org/literature/book/the-encyclopedia-of-human-computer-interaction-2nd-ed/wearable-computing>, accessed 19 July 2016.

Mann, S. (2014) 'Maktivism: Authentic making for technology in the service of humanity', in M. Ratto & M. Boler (eds.) *DIY Citizenship*. Cambridge, MA: MIT Press, pp. 29–51.

Marcuse, H. (1998) *Technology, War and Fascism*. London: Routledge.

Markoff, J. (2016) 'Creating a computer voice that people like', *New York Times*, 14 February, <https://www.nytimes.com/2016/02/15/technology/creating-a-computer-voice-that-people-like.html>, accessed 27 March 2017.

Marres, N. (2014) 'The environmental teapot and other loaded household objects', in P. Harvey et al. (eds.) *Objects and Materials: A Routledge Companion*. London: Routledge, pp. 260–71.

Masunaga, S. (2016) 'Here are some of the tweets that got Microsoft's AI

Tay in trouble', *Los Angeles Times*, 25 March, <http://www.latimes.com/business/technology/la-fi-tn-microsoft-tay-tweets-20160325-htmlstory.html>, accessed 26 January 2017.

Mathiesen, T. (1997) 'The viewer society: Michel Foucault's "panopticon" revisited', *Theoretical Criminology*, vol. 1, no. 2, pp. 215–34.

McAuliffe S. (2017) 'Inner voice', in M. Bunz, B. M. Kaiser & K. Thiele (eds.) *Symptoms of our Planetary Condition*. Lüneburg: Meson Press, pp. 73–7.

McChesney, R. W. & Nichols, J. (2016) *People Get Ready*. New York: Nation Books.

McLuhan, M. (1964) *Understanding Media*. London: Routledge.

McLuhan, M. & Fiore, Q. (1967) *The Medium is the Massage*. San Francisco: Hardwired.

McQuail, D. (1997) *Audience Analysis*. Thousand Oaks, CA: Sage.

Meikle, G. (2002) *Future Active*. New York: Routledge.

Meikle, G. (2008) 'Electronic civil disobedience and symbolic power', in A. Karatzogianni (ed.) *Cyber-Conflict and Global Politics*. London: Routledge, pp. 177–87.

Meikle, G. (2016) *Social Media*. New York: Routledge.

Meikle, G. & Young, S. (2012) *Media Convergence*. Basingstoke: Palgrave Macmillan.

Microsoft Bot Framework (2016) 'Build a great conversationalist', <https://dev.botframework.com>, accessed 26 January 2017.

Miller, D. (2010) *Stuff*. Cambridge: Polity.

Mordvintsev, A., Olah, C. & Tyka, M. (2015) 'Inceptionism: Going deeper into neural networks', *Google Research Blog*, 17 June, <https://research.googleblog.com/2015/06/inceptionism-going-deeper-into-neural.html>, accessed 26 January 2017.

Mosco, V. (2014) *To the Cloud*. Boulder, CO: Paradigm.

Mukisa, S. (2015) '#google maps needs a night mode so that it doesn't try to send you through a dark unlit park late at night!', *Twitter*, 24 October, <https://twitter.com/skmukisa/status/658046035441401856>, accessed 16 February 2017.

Murray, J. H. (1997) *Hamlet on the Holodeck*. Cambridge, MA: MIT Press.

Nafus, D. (2016) 'Introduction', in D. Nafus (ed.) *Quantified*. Cambridge, MA: MIT Press, pp. ix–xxxi.

Nass, C. I. & Brave, S. (2005) *Wired for Speech*. Cambridge, MA: MIT Press.

Neff, G. & Nafus, D. (2016) *Self-Tracking*. Cambridge, MA: MIT Press.

Negri, R. (2017) 'Stranded 6 miles from home', *Instagram*, 14 January, <https://www.instagram.com/p/BPQeu9VDDCI/>, accessed 16 February 2017.

Negroponte, N. (1995) *Being Digital*. London: Hodder and Stoughton.

Newitz, A. (2015a) 'Ashley Madison code shows more women, and more bots', *Gizmodo*, 31 August, <http://gizmodo.com/ashley-madison-code-shows-more-women-and-more-bots-1727613924>, accessed 16 August 2016.

Newitz, A. (2015b) 'How Ashley Madison hid its fembot con from users and investigators', *Gizmodo*, 8 September, <http://gizmodo.com/how-ashley-madison-hid-its-fembot-con-from-users-and-in-1728410265>, accessed 16 August 2016.

Nissenbaum, H. & Patterson, H. (2016) 'Biosensing in context: Health privacy in a connected world', in D. Nafus (ed.) *Quantified*. Cambridge, MA: MIT Press, pp. 79–100.

Ofcom (2016) 'Adults' media use and attitudes', April, <https://www.ofcom.org.uk/__data/assets/pdf_file/0026/80828/2016-adults-media-use-and-attitudes.pdf>, accessed 26 January 2017.

Olsen, E. (2013) Scientists uncover invisible motion in video', *New York Times*, 27 February, <http://bits.blogs.nytimes.com/2013/02/27/scientists-uncover-invisible-motion-in-video>, accessed 26 January 2017.

O'Neil, C. (2016) *Weapons of Math Destruction: How Big Data Increases Inequality and Threatens Democracy*. London: Penguin.

O'Reilly, T. (2005) 'What is Web 2.0', *O'Reilly Media*, 30 September, <http://www.oreilly.com/pub/a//web2/archive/what-is-web-20.html>, accessed 1 June 2016.

Özkul, D. (2015) 'Mobile communication technologies and spatial perception: Mapping London,' in R. Wilken & G. Goggin (eds.) *Locative Media*. London: Routledge, pp. 39–51.

Pennebaker, J. W. (2013) *The Secret Life of Pronouns*. New York: Bloomsbury Press.

Petrov, S. (2016) 'Announcing SyntaxNet: The world's most accurate parser goes open source', *Google Research Blog*, 12 May, <https://research.googleblog.com/2016/05/announcing-syntaxnet-worlds-most.html>, accessed 26 January 2017.

Pew Research Center (2014) 'The Internet of Things will thrive by 2025', 14 May, <http://www.pewinternet.org/2014/05/14/internet-of-things>, accessed 30 August 2016.

Pew Research Center (2017) 'The Internet of Things Connectivity Binge: What Are the Implications?' 6 June, <http://www.pewinternet.org/2017/06/06/the-internet-of-things-connectivity-binge-what-are-the-implications>, accessed 21 June 2017.

Photonic Fence (n.d.) 'Intellectual Ventures Laboratory', <http://www.intellectualventureslab.com/work/photonic-fence>, accessed 26 January 2017.

Potts, J. (2015) *The New Time and Space*. Basingstoke: Palgrave Macmillan.

Rettberg, J. W. (2014) *Seeing Ourselves Through Technology*. Basingstoke: Palgrave Macmillan.

Rich, E. & Miah, A. (2016) 'Mobile, wearable and ingestible health technologies: Towards a critical research agenda', *Health Sociology Review*, vol. 26, no. 1, pp. 84–97.

Rose, D. (2014) *Enchanted Objects*. New York: Scribner.

Ross, A. (1994) 'The new smartness', in G. Bender & T. Druckrey (eds.) *Culture on the Brink*. Seattle, WA: Bay Press, pp. 329–41.

Sauter, M. (2014) *The Coming Swarm*. London: Bloomsbury.

Schneier, B. (2016a) 'The Internet of Things will turn large-scale hacks into real world disasters', *Motherboard*, 25 July, <https://motherboard.vice.com/read/the-internet-of-things-will-cause-the-first-ever-large-scale-internet-disaster>, accessed 4 November 2016.

Schneier, B. (2016b) 'Someone is learning how to take down the Internet', *Schneier on Security*, 13 September, <https://www.schneier.com/essays/archives/2016/09/someone_is_learning_.html>, accessed 2 November 2016.

Schröder, S. (2017) 'Tesla owner gets stranded in the desert after relying on phone to start the car', *Mashable*, 16 January, <http://mashable.com/2017/01/16/tesla-stranded-phone-keys/#se7zVSKqFZqb>, accessed 28 January 2017.

Schuppli, S. (2014) 'Deadly algorithms: Can legal codes hold software accountable for code that kills?', *Radical Philosophy*, no. 187, pp. 2–8.

Schuppli, S. (2017) 'Computing the law / searching for justice', in M. Hlavajova & S. Sheikh (eds.) *Former West: Art and the Contemporary after 1989*. Cambridge, MA: MIT Press.

Share Lab (2015) 'Invisible infrastructures: Mobile permissions', 2 March, <http://labs.rs/en/invisible-infrastructures-mobile-permissions>, accessed 27 March 2017.

Shaviro, S. (2014) *The Universe of Things*. Minneapolis, MN: University of Minnesota Press.

Shelton, M., Rainie, L. & Madden, M. (2015) 'Americans' privacy strategies post-Snowden', *Pew Research Center*, 15 March, <http://www.pewinternet.org/2015/03/16/Americans-Privacy-Strategies-Post-Snowden>, accessed 26 January 2017.

Silverman, C. (2015) '7 creepy baby monitor stories that will terrify all parents', *BuzzFeed*, 24 July, <https://www.buzzfeed.com/craigsilverman/creeps-hack-baby-monitors-and-say-terrifying-thing>, accessed 10 February 2017.

Simondon, G. (2012) 'Technical mentality', in A. Boever, A. Murray, J. Roffe & A. Woodward (eds.) *Gilbert Simondon: Being and Technology*. Edinburgh: Edinburgh University Press, pp. 1–15.

Simondon, G. (2017) *On the Mode of Existence of Technical Objects*, translated by C. Malaspina. Minneapolis, MN: Univocal Publishing.

Singhal, A. (2011) 'Knocking down barriers to knowledge', *Google Official Blog*, 14 June, <https://googleblog.blogspot.co.uk/2011/06/knocking-down-barriers-to-knowledge.html>, accessed 25 January 2017.

Singhal, A. (2012) 'Introducing the knowledge graph: Things, not strings', *Google Official Blog*, 16 May, <https://googleblog.blogspot.co.uk/2012/05/introducing-knowledge-graph-things-not.html>, accessed 25 January 2017.

Soderlind, L. (2016) '.@googlemaps directs me to walk thru a dark park at night – maybe there should be a button for women who prefers avoiding dicey shortcuts?', *Twitter*, 3 June, <https://twitter.com/LauraSoderlind/status/738662112080187392>, accessed 16 February 2017.

Solon, O. (2016a) 'The rise of robots: Forget evil AI – the real risk is far more insidious', *The Guardian*, 30 August, <https://www.theguardian.com/technology/2016/aug/30/rise-of-robots-evil-artificial-intelligence-uc-berkeley>, accessed 25 January 2017.

Solon, O. (2016b) 'Lidar: The self-driving technology that could help Tesla avoid another tragedy', *The Guardian*, 6 July, <https://www.theguardian.com/technology/2016/jul/06/lidar-self-driving-technology-tesla-crash-elon-musk>, accessed 28 January 2017.

Srnicek, N. & Williams, A. (2015) *Inventing the Future*. London: Verso.

Stafford-Fraser, Q. (n.d.) 'The Trojan Room coffee pot resources', <http://www.cl.cam.ac.uk/coffee/qsf/index.html>, accessed 9 June 2016.

Sterling, B. (2005) *Shaping Things*. Cambridge, MA: MIT Press.

Sterling, B. (2014) *The Epic Struggle of the Internet of Things*. Moscow: Strelka Press.

Sutton-Smith, B. (1997) *The Ambiguity of Play*. Cambridge, MA: Harvard University Press.

Szegedy, C. (2014) 'Building a deeper understanding of images', *Google Research Blog*, 5 September, <https://research.googleblog.com/2014/09/building-deeper-understanding-of-images.html#uds-search-results>, accessed 26 January 2017.

Taylor, E. (2016) 'Supermarket self-checkouts and retail theft: The curious case of the SWIPERS', *Criminology and Criminal Justice*, vol. 16, no. 5, pp. 552–67.

Tesco (2015) 'Tesco to end "unexpected item in the bagging area" ', *Tesco News Releases*, 30 July, <https://www.tescoplc.com/news/

news-releases/2015/tesco-to-end-unexpected-item-in-the-bagging-area>, accessed 26 January 2017.

Tesla (2016a) 'Tesla press information, Model S', <https://www.tesla.com/ presskit/autopilot#models>, accessed 7 December 2016.

Tesla (2016b) 'A tragic loss', 30 June, <https://www.tesla.com/blog/tragic-loss>, accessed 7 December 2016.

Thrift, N. (2004) 'Remembering the technological unconscious by foregrounding knowledges of position', *Environment and Planning D: Society and Space*, vol. 22, no. 1, pp. 175–90.

Tickle, P. (2014) 'That moment when Google Maps take you down a lane or into a park and you wish there was a "walking alone at night" setting. #YesAllWomen', *Twitter*, 12 June, <https://twitter.com/pollytext/ status/477005168072859648>, accessed 16 February 2017.

Till, C. (2014) 'Exercise as LABOUR: Quantified self and the transformation of exercise into labour', *Societies*, vol. 4, no. 3, pp. 446–62.

Trinidad, D. [YoungPTone] (2016) 'HR reading consistently high last few days', *reddit.com/r/fitbit*, 4 February, <https://www.reddit.com/r/fitbit/ comments/445ppj/hr_reading_consistently_high_last_few_days>, accessed 3 January 2017.

Turing, A. M. (1999 [1950]) 'Computing machinery and intelligence', in P. A. Mayer (ed.) *Computer Media and Communication: A Reader*. Oxford: Oxford University Press, pp. 37–58.

Turkle, S. (1995) *Life on the Screen*. London: Phoenix.

Urmson, C. (2016a) 'The view from the front seat of the Google self-driving car, chapter 4', *Medium*, 16 January, <https://medium.com/@ chris_urmson/the-view-from-the-front-seat-of-the-google-self-driving-car-chapter-4-d707b9e925d3#.phgjwcx6v>, accessed 26 January 2017.

Urmson, C. (2016b) 'Google self-driving car project', *SXSW Interactive*, 12 March, <https://www.youtube.com/watch?v=Uj-rK8V-rik>, accessed 26 January 2017.

Virilio, P. (1989) *War and Cinema*. London: Verso.

Virilio, P. & Lotringer, S. (1983) *Pure War*. New York: Semiotext(e).

Wang, D. (2007) 'Stuck in traffic?', *Google Official Blog*, 28 February, <https:// googleblog.blogspot.co.uk/2007/02/stuck-in-traffic.html>, accessed 26 January 2017.

Wark, M. (2012) *Telesthesia*. Cambridge: Polity.

Warren, S. D. & Brandeis, L. D. (1890) 'The right to privacy', *Harvard Law Review*, vol. IV, no. 5, <http://www.jjllplaw.com/The-Right-to-Privacy-Warren-Brandeis-Harvard-Law-Review-1890.html>, accessed 30 January 2017.

Warwick, K. (2012) *Artificial Intelligence*. London: Routledge.

Waseem, Z., Davidson, T., Warmsley, D. & Weber, I. (2017) 'Understanding abuse: A typology of abusive language detection subtasks', accepted paper for the 'First Workshop on Abusive Language Online', The Association for Computational Linguistics, 24 August.

Waymo (2016) 'Building maps for a self-driving car', *Medium*, <https://medium.com/waymo/building-maps-for-a-self-driving-car-723b4d9cd3f4#.itm09dewv>, accessed 28 January 2017.

Weiser, M. (1991) 'The computer for the 21st century', *Scientific American*, September, pp. 94–104.

Weizenbaum, J. (1966) 'ELIZA – a computer program for the study of natural language communication between man and machine', *Communications of the ACM*, vol. 9, no. 1, pp. 36–45.

Weizenbaum, J. (2003 [1976]) 'From *Computer Power and Human Reason*', in N. Wardrip-Fruin & N. Montfort (eds.) *The New Media Reader*. Cambridge, MA: MIT Press, pp. 367–75.

Whitson, J. R. (2013) 'Gaming the quantified self', *Surveillance & Society*, vol. 11, nos. 1–2, pp. 163–76.

Williams, H. (2016) 'Microsoft's teen chatbot has gone wild', *Gizmodo*, 25 March, <http://www.gizmodo.com.au/2016/03/microsofts-teen-chatbot-has-gone-wild>, accessed 26 January 2017.

Williams, R. (1974) *Television: Technology and Cultural Form*. London: Fontana.

Winner, L. (1986) *The Whale and the Reactor*. Chicago: University of Chicago Press.

Wittgenstein, L. (2009) *Philosophical Investigations*, translated by G. E. M. Anscombe, P. M. S. Hacker & J. Schulte. Chichester: John Wiley.

Wodak, R. (ed.) (2013) *Critical Discourse Analysis: Concepts, History, Theory*. London: Sage.

Wolf, G. (2016) 'The quantified self: Reverse engineering', in D. Nafus (ed.) *Quantified*. Cambridge, MA: MIT Press, pp. 67–72.

Woolf, N. (2016) 'DDoS attack that disrupted internet was largest of its kind in history, experts say', *The Guardian*, 26 October, <https://www.theguardian.com/technology/2016/oct/26/ddos-attack-dyn-mirai-botnet>, accessed 4 November 2016.

Zamen, W. (2009) 'HP computers are racist', *YouTube*, 10 December, <https://www.youtube.com/watch?v=t4DT3tQqgRM>, accessed 15 December 2016.

Zuckerberg, M. (2016) 'Building Jarvis', *Facebook*, 19 December, <https://www.facebook.com/notes/mark-zuckerberg/building-jarvis/10154361492931634>, accessed 26 January 2017.

Index